Illinois Central College
Learning Resources Center

# Greenhorns

Paula (Anna Karina) juxtaposed with Walt Disney figures and U.S. travel posters (page 100 of text).

pierian press 1982

# Greenhorns

## Foreign Filmmakers Interpret America

By Norman Kagan

ISBN 0-87650-143-9
LC 82-81470

The Pierian Press
P.O. Box 1808
Ann Arbor, MI 48106

to my mother
**Rush Kagan**
and to the memory of my father
**Simon R. Kagan**
wise, brave, and gentle

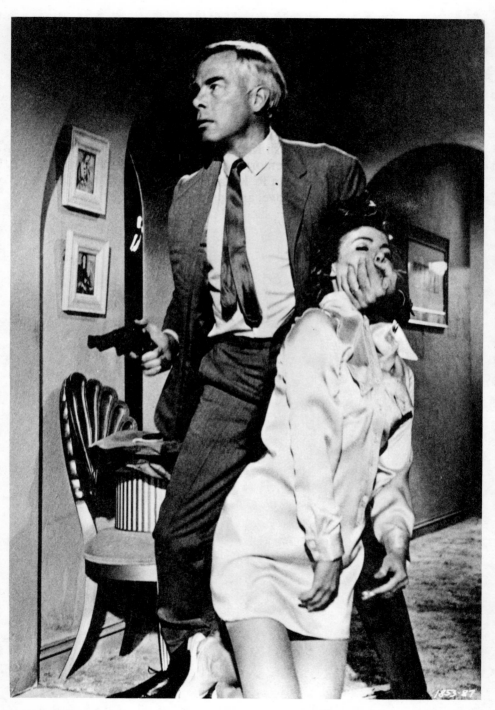

Walker (Lee Marvin) overwhelms his treacherous betraying wife Lynne (Sharon Acker) (page 25 of text).

# Contents

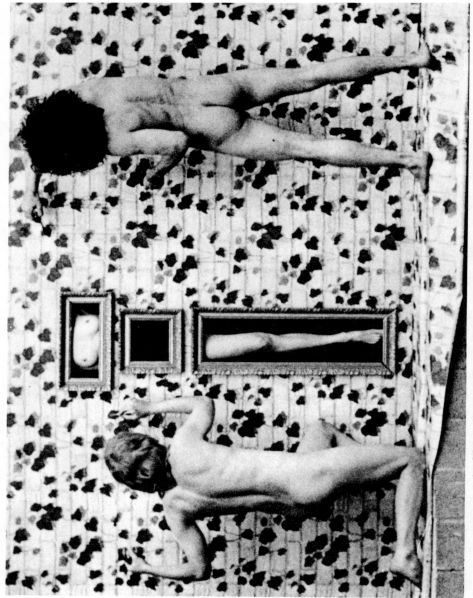

Art History V: The lions as modernist abstracted forms (page 138 of text).

# Illustrations

# Foreword

Norman Kagan involves us, in these pages, in a most absorbing and challenging game. He confronts us with interpretations of the American scene by non-American film directors. The selected group is diverse in background, but all are *auteur* directors of distinguished achievement and high standing, whose work regularly reflects their personal visions. They were in control of what they were doing. We can assume that the films reflect, to a considerable extent, their impressions of us.

All this will provide much food for thought, and raises more questions than it can possibly answer. To what extent has the American scene become a living Rorschach inkblot in which the foreign film maker can readily see the world problems that trouble him? To what extent is he feeding back into our film world ideas about America that Hollywood itself has disseminated, and perhaps set in motion? To what extent do the films represent widely held views abroad about America? Precise answers to such questions are obviously not possible. Meanwhile, they are worth pondering.

From the beginning of film history, America has regularly been pictured by foreign film artists newly arrived on our shores, as our burgeoning film industry drew artists from other lands. There have also been countless films about America by film makers who were never here. In an appendix Norman Kagan gives us a list — tentative and incomplete but none the less valuable and fascinating — of "greenhorn" films, ranging from famous to obscure, and representing all decades of film history. But the seven features on which the book mainly focuses are of recent vintage. All are from the 1960s and 1970s and deal with what can be considered contemporary culture.

They represent a particular chapter in American film annals. About mid-century the big-studio system, the monopolistic structure that had dominated the film world for decades, began to come apart, and films by foreign film makers began capturing a growing share of American screentime and film revenue. The Hollywood "majors" were meanwhile shifting their main emphasis to distribution and investment, leaving many of the risks of production to independents, always in search of capital. The majors accordingly coopted the foreign threat by absorbing it into their range of enterprise. It is notable that most of the films in this volume, although made by foreigners, were the product of American finance.

They reflect a turbulent world. Many of the themes can be found also in the films of other lands: migrations to the cities, derelicts in the cities, corruption, exploitation, drugs, shifting sexual mores, group tensions and explosions, the generation gap, an erosion of the borderline between "legitimate" and underground enterprise. If in these films we see these matters in an American context, this is an inevitable result of America's dominant standing in the world. The eyes of the world are on us.

Norman Kagan has focused on an impressive group of artists. He has described the circumstances under which each of the films was made. Because many of them are not readily available to readers, he has given us an impressionistic synopsis of each, to convey something of its color and ambiance as well as its structure. Finally he provides comments by the film makers themselves, and his own cogent analyses.

No country has sat for its film portrait more often — and more willingly and permissively — than the United States. Here is an intriguing look at the experience — and an original and challenging contribution to current film literature.

Erik Barnouw

# Introduction

As the Addendum suggests, there is a long history of foreign filmmakers using their craft to comment on, criticize, or otherwise probe the United States (or, to rephrase a Latin American designation, the "collossus of celluloid"). In some cases, starting with the German expatriates of the 1930s, the creators in fact commenced dissecting America on arrival in Hollywood. Though there are a few books on the lives of those expatriates, I believe this is the first survey of the much larger subject.

Because the subject is so vast, the research problems are equally large — numbers of films, comprehending foreign cultural contexts, unavailability of prints. On the other hand, commentary in certain categories, notably the Vietnam era films, is sometimes extensive. For this reason, I chose to exclude several types of works; major cross-cultural "art" films (e.g., **Last Tango in Paris, The Passenger**), stylish political thrillers (**State of Siege, Punishment Park**), transposed American genre films (**A Fistful of Dollars, The Bad Sleep Well**), and works secure in film history (**Shadow of a Doubt, Greed**). Rather, I have chosen works equally rich in political and social commentary, but less explicitly so. Like the protagonist in **The Quiet American**, these directors are "not involved."

In the mid-sixties, critic Vincent Canby wrote an article for the Sunday *New York Times* entitled "Foreign Filmmakers — Do They All Hate Us?" It was of course written at the height of the Vietnam War, but the question it raises leads into others that are still important: How do other nations see the United States? How do they interpret our characteristic works — the crime thriller, the film dealing with outcast/outlaws, the youth movie? How would they portray our business society, our self-absorbed behavior, or our fascination with our own media? The films I have chosen to discuss deal with these ongoing forms and subjects, hence may be more worthy of critical analysis than stylish or topical or revolutionary films. Each chapter consists of a production history, a brief treatment, a critique of the film's social comments, and a reflection on these by the director.

# Acknowledgements

My special thanks to Brian Camp of E.F.L.A., Professor Milos Forman of Columbia University, Norman Kaplan of Metro Goldwyn Mayer, Robert L. Oppenheim of Columbia Pictures, Charles Saltzman of Eyr Programs, Charles Silver of the Museum of Modern Art Film Study Center, Jean Valier of the French Institute, Ms. Ingrid Scheib-Rothebart of Goethe House, Professor Erik Barnouw, and to Professor Michael Kerbel, who had a very good idea.

Thanks also for courtesy and cooperation extended by Metro Goldwyn Mayer, Columbia Pictures, Eyr Programs, United Artists, Universal Pictures, Cinememorabilia, Movie Star News, and the Museum of Modern Art Film Stills Collection.

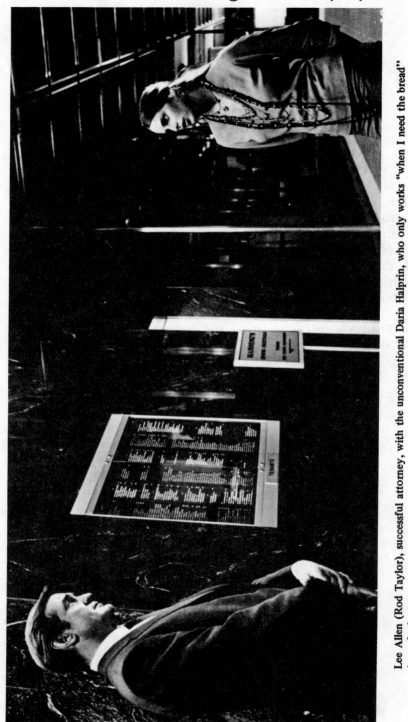

Lee Allen (Rod Taylor), successful attorney, with the unconventional Daria Halprin, who only works "when I need the bread" (page 3 of text).

# Michaelangelo Antonioni

# ZABRISKIE POINT

Antonioni decided to shoot his first American film for a number
of reasons. He wanted to get out of Italy ("Get rid of my milieu");
he already had visited America and been fascinated by it as a place
where the contradictions visible in modern life everywhere were
already clashing. Now he crisscrossed the country, delighting in the
landscape — he chose Death Valley because it is so beautiful, not
because it is dead — and found a good story idea about the same
time, a clipping about a teenager who stole a private plane and was
shot trying to return it. As usual, Antonioni collaborated on the
script, working with both Italians (Tonino Guerra, Clare Peplo) and
natives (Sam Shepard, Fred Garner) on what he calls the several
faces of the film.

Production presented special problems: the American crew
wasn't used to Antonioni's technique of improvising, and wanted a
schedule worked out for the next day. Antonioni just couldn't do
that: "It just depends on my mood — I think that to improvise as I
did in this film is to be biographical: I put in this film my daily
mood." (1.5)

Antonioni's technique varied through the film. In the opening
with the young radicals, he gave some themes he wanted them to
talk around, and some definite lines, but outside of that, they were
free. Then he shot the sequence several times over a week, and
edited it down, partly for good visuals, mostly for good dialectic.

Working with Rod Taylor proved easy and straightforward, the
techniques of the two professionals meshing effectively.

From Daria Halprin and Mark Frechette he wanted a different
kind of performance. Instead of using them as actors, he tried to provoke them into being themselves; Mark's rebellion is as pure and
colorful as the film itself; Daria free but a little bourgeois, a character who is changed by what happens. Antonioni sees her meeting
with the Indian girl as motivating her final departure, making it clear
she could not stay. For the Indian girl is Daria's age, and she would
be like her "living in" and working for the owners of the house.

"Suddenly, she couldn't do it." (1.5)

One of Antonioni's post-release comments seems a good guide for reading this abbreviated treatment:

> "Of course, I didn't say everything that can be said about America. My film only touches on just a few themes, a few places. Somebody can say this is missing or that is missing . . . The story is certainly a simple one. Nonetheless, the content is actually very complex. It is not a question of reading between the lines, but one of reading between the images." (1.6)

In soft golden light, young black and white student radicals argue silently, in quick cuts from face to face, over electronic music like soft angelic moans, a three-four knocking heartbeat, a rattlesnake hissing. Titles in modern print. The voices cut through in flat echoing fragments, expressions in quick scissored cuts: intelligent, intense, troubled, dubious. The gold haze vanishes. We see not-so-pretty radicals, Frank Boardalke of Stop-the-Draft, a regal Catherine Cleaver.

A loud belligerent black voice bangs: "You just go *back* and tell them this motherfucker is closed *down, on strike, Jack!*" Shouts of approval.

A girl wants to stop ROTC. The black tells her sarcastically: "All you gotta *do* is go to the *ROTC* building, take a *bottle*, fill it full of *gasoline*, plug it with a *rag* — "

What if you want to end sociology?

Disgusted: "White radicalism is a mixture of bullshit and jive!"

A girl claims there are plenty of potential white revolutionaries.

The black: "You dig pigs bustin' you on your *head*, kickin' down your *door*, stoppin' you from *living'*, you can't get a *job*, can't go to *school*, can't *eat* — that's what makes you a revolutionary — dig!"

The girl's clear voice: that's fine for blacks — but what will make white people into revolutionaries?

A moment of silence, then the argument swirls off: "This school is gonna be closed down, *period!*"

The argument drifts into tactics: do they have enough support? form attack squads? use cars as barricades? "How about your car?" someone asks. All laugh.

A dubious voice: "Are you willing to die?"

"Black people *are* dying. Black people gained this leadership in *blood*, Jack — we ain't gonna give it up."

A hawkfaced young man, Mark (Mark Frechette), announces loudly, self-consciously: "I'm willing to die too . . . "

Faces turn towards him: questioning, skeptical.

2

Softer, shrugging: " . . . but not of boredom." He walks out.

Grins, smirks. Angrily: What is this, meetings aren't his trip! A revolutionary has to work with other people.

The black in a worldly voice: "Teach him the first stage, a revolutionary party. That bourgeois individualism — it's gonna get him killed!"

The crowd surges approval . . .

In the echoing modernistic lobby of an office building, a lovely long-legged girl trips toward the security post, dark hair down her back, love beads at her throat. The guard looks up from his TV monitors.

Daria (Daria Halprin), in a rich contralto: "Is the door open to the roof? Can I go up?"

The man balks: "Why don't you eat in the cafeteria?"

She shrugs, sighs as handsome businessman Lee Allen (Rod Taylor) strides up. Smiling, she explains.

"You do secretarial work?"

"It's not something I really dig to do. I just work when I need the bread." . . . .

An old red pickup truck zips noisily through the industrial slums of Los Angeles: past an enormous billboard, in the style of 1890s prints, of a hog farmer tossing corn to his sows. Mark is driving, his mustached roommate at his side. Helmeted motorcycle cops roar past; Mark gives the finger.

To weird electronic tinkles, horns, screeches, hisses, they race past piles of scrap, tumbles of waste, big signs announcing production plants. With a squeal of brakes, Mark cuts off a convertible; a pretty girl waves.

"A girl from my long gone past," Mark laments. "Alice . . . my sister."

The roommate is filling out a form for early release. "You have to be realistic."

"Look, man, the day you don't count on losing is the day I'll join the movement," Mark argues.

"For lots it's survival, not choice."

"That's what I mean," Mark mutters. "It's serious, not a game. . . I'm tired of it, man, kids rappin' about violence, cops doin' it . . . people only act when they need to — and I need to sooner than that."

They swing up to the curb, the roommate joins a picketline in front of the university . . .

Intent faces, electronics cabinets, uniforms: a police command post. "Control one to control five," rasps a voice. Mark is at the window with a bald, bored cop:

"One of the colleges? Being booked now . . . maybe five minutes,

3

Mark (Mark Frechette) and Bill (Bruce Nickles) discuss a gun purchase with a salesman.

maybe five hours."

Mark wanders into the complex. A whistling police helicopter lifts off, dazzling highlights glinting. Dark buses with grilled windows, full of young people, rush bumping down a ramp, leading Mark to the booking area, full of sometimes bloody radicals. A bearded, chubby professor is frisked and booked by a humorless cop, "Occupation?"

"Associate Professor of History."

"That's too long, Bill. Just put down 'clerk.' "

Mark, at a barred door, waves. The kids grin. A cop snarls to move on: "Now you get a chance to see your friend!" Mark is jerked inside, manhandled against a grill, frisked, booked: "Name?"

"Karl Marx." The clerk types out Carl . . . .

Mark and roommate enter a gunshop, displaying hundreds of weapons on walls, racks, circular stands, muzzles everywhere.

Mark, low: "Our neighborhood is . . . borderline. We've got to protect our women."

"I'll see you don't go defenseless," the man answers, handing out pistols. The boys inspect them casually, opening the cylinders, peering in the muzzles . . . .

Another shop, another arsenal. "One other thing about the law," the boys are told, packages under their arms, "If you shoot 'em in the backyard, be sure you drag 'em inside . . . "

A plastic beach ball jumps from one smirking plastic doll to another around a toy pool. A rich fruity voice: "The total relaxation of desert living . . . "

Around the TV screen, the tough-faced promoters of Sunnydunes Estates peer at a tape of a commercial: rigid plastic folk playing golf on a fibre-glass lawn, a polystyrene father and son shoot a papier–mache quail. "Stop driving yourself crazy in that miserable crowded city . . . " The masters of the new life study the rigid, madly grinning shapes on the screen . . .

An air-conditioned limousine slips through the frenetic Los Angeles traffic. The radio gabbles about the heat, Vietnam, student riots. Lee Allen drives, talking only of Sunnydunes . . .

The same report, with no transition, echoes through the big old rooms where Mark hovers over his radio. An American flag, dyed red, hangs in a corner. Mark suddenly jumps: "I've got to go down there and see for myself!"

He shoves the pistol inside his boot, emerges from the rundown, converted old brick firehouse, drives the pickup off through the deteriorated neighborhood . . .

The limousine shoots up to the soaring tower of Sunnydunes Development. Lee Allen and associate trot towards the entrance, swinging briefcases. Inside, stock quotations run on an overhead

**5**

display, a computer blinks through a glass wall, Muzak violins tremble, business machines clack away. A stocky, walrus-mustached adman stands up beside his tape machine as Lee Allen strides through to the group's greetings . . .

Guitars and fiddles twang and race from a brilliant blue sky as a pearly old Chevy with whitewalls takes a climbing turn off a desert highway. A smiling, enormous-eyed Daria studies her map below a billboard of a clear salad bowl filled with greenbacks and silver.

In his office, Lee studies reports while a screen blinks time-zoned clock faces. At his back, a window wall shows a soaring, brooding black tower dominating the cityscape, decorated with gargoyles and terraces. An American flag flaps beyond. Small cacti and desert plants, frozen in styrene blocks, decorate his elaborate desk. Annoyed about Daria, he has her home paged. His blunt, powerful face dominates the screen.

"Goodbye?" asks a mild young voice.

Allen, blindly: "What? Hello, do you know where I can reach Daria? . . . She left? . . . Do you mind telling me who this is?"

"Yeah, I mind . . . hello." The phone clicks.

Frustrated, Allen turns on the hushed, audacious voices: "Development of a million acres . . . a five billion dollar expenditure . . . well, we can handle *that*."

From a low angle, Allen is powerful, petulant, massive, a flag rippling beyond. The composition makes the pondering executive into an inglorious brooding Lincoln . . .

A line of truculent police in visored helmets glare (this footage was shot live at San Francisco State). The enormous line, weirdly proportioned by a wide-angle lens, curves ominously across a university lawn, drifts forward. A crowd of students yells, mills. Suddenly the cops plunge, yelling and screaming, the mass of students sags back, routs. From inside a ravaged building, the camera peers through cratered windows at cops with raging truncheons. A bloody student stumbles through the crowd, pawing at a red face. A shiny patrol car, domelight and bleeper working, shoots into a parking lot, pirouettes. From it leap visored minions with riot guns. A knot of excited students chameleons against a wall as cops run by. Mark dashes past a building brightly labelled Liberal Arts, in silvery letters.

Police crouch before a library, rifles and pistols aimed. Inside, the pleasant reading room is deserted; books, magazines, papers litter the floor. The squatting, sweating cops bullhorn: "If you don't throw your weapons out and give up, we'll get you out by other means . . . "

Silence.

A hissing conference, a spinning, sputtering gas grenade crashes

6

through a holed glass door. Gas pours out thickly. Choking, four blacks stumble clear, arms raised, sprawling flat on command. At once, a fifth lurches clear, staggering, pistol high.

"He's got a gun!" CRUMP! The black shape topples, blood-spotted.

Mark presses himself to a wall, body in marksman position, pistol out.

Another blast; Mark covers his face as the killer cop flops forward.

In a long tracking shop, Mark flees across silent perfect lawns . . .

In a green light, a crowded city bus; fat black and white hausfraus, crabby-looking kids, aimless old men. The bus hisses: end of the line.

Outside, Mark's sunglasses off, air hot, city dead flat, streets crowded with cottagey banks, gas stations, used car lots. Mark furtively enters a deli and calls home as two men in coveralls ask thickly for sandwiches. "You want extra, you pay extra," the fat proprietor admonishes them darkly.

The mustached roommate warns thin-voiced: "Better cool it, somebody said they saw you on TV . . . on the news this guy looked just like you . . . " Mark hangs up suddenly.

The workingman and owner laugh nastily. Mark asks to be trusted for the price of a sandwich.

"It's not that I don't trust you," the man shrugs lugubriously, "but if I trusted you, I'd have to trust everybody in the whole world."

"Yeah," Mark mumbles sourly.

Outside, traffice noises hiss at a bewildered Mark, punctuated by a private plane's buzz. Enormous billboards close off the sky: *Fly United to New York*; a family peers from Liberty's torch. Used cars in shabby formation, an Official Smog Inspection Station, a diner with dirty white paint. Mark watches another monoplane's descent. A fire engine wangs stridently by.

The young man slips onto the field through a half open gate. Shot: Two arguing businessmen in a cockpit, inaudible for the whistling props. The small aircraft shimmers in the heat. Mark chooses a single engine painted bright pink: Lilly Seven. He glances about, squeezes in, touches the buttons. As he guns the motor, it coughs and roars, the prop spins invisible. Lilly Seven rolls out. Mark grins, eyes slitted, and accelerates Lilly Seven, engine humming.

In the tower, dead calm while a voice gabbles crisply: "Lilly Seven — Lilly-Seven abort ⊥ your — takeoff — traffice-moving — in — opposite — direction!" A grinning Mark zooms over the approaching lander, disappearing upwards to the quick light sounds of guitars, bells and electronic hums in "Dark Star." Suburban tracts sweep to the horizon: homes freeways looping, clumps of offices, more speckles of homes saturate the earth, mazes and labyrinths, an omnivorous, all-powerful standardizing pattern. Mark climbs above it . . .

To guitars, flutes, voices, Daria drives the old dove-gray Chevy across the gray wastes munching a bright apple . . .

In the board room, Sunnydunes executives wrangle over contingency figures and blasting rock slopes. Lee Allen takes a call in his office . . .

Daria, earnest and sensual, is calling from a desert tavern, looking for a town that sounds like Blairville, Valleyville, something —

Allen switches the phone to loudspeaker and whips out his Atlas. Querulously: "Have you got someone to meet?"

It's a fantastic place for meditation; Daris replies: "You *think* about things." She cuts him off as he tries to find her out . . .

The barman tells her that she's standing in Hollister, and the boy she's looking for is there ruining "a piece of American history."

A rheumy-eyed old man sits quavering: "I was middle-weight champion of the world in 1920."

Daria's friend brought emotionally disturbed kids to the desert. Barkeep: "But if *Los Angeles* don't wannem, why should we wannem!"

A stone shatters the front window and he curses. The jukebox plays the melancholy "Tennessee Waltz."

The roadside desertscape is shabby, empty. A couple of young boys hide behind an old box, then run off as Daria approaches. Another, dreamyfaced and sad, picks at the wires of a broken piano. "Hey kid, where's Jimmy?" The gentle-faced boy turns away.

Daria follows the others to a wide abandoned platform. The shabby boys climb up after her, yelling, surround her, pushing awkwardly, half shy, half knowing: "Can we have a piece of ass?" They grab and pull at her, but she slaps them off, squealing, runs to the car. The old boxer, awash in the nostalgic song, placidly watches her drive off. The melancholy "Tennessee Waltz" drifts on . . .

The sound track thumps into the virile roar of Lilly Seven. Mark follows a railroad line across the desert, swift tiny shadow racing down the track through dirty yellow sand and dark green scrub, across a moaning Diesel-pulled freight. Mark waves . . .

Daria brakes the Chevy to a silent stop . . . and Mark arcs loudly across the bright blue, as she stoops to get radiator water from a colored tank, her dark hair over her shoulders down her back. The trajectory of the plane cuts the curve of the highway once, twice, Daria drives on . . .

Above, Mark circles and swoops for the ground as Daria chews her gum and peers ahead. From behind, Lilly Seven races up almost brushing her roof. Excited, self-conscious, Daria: "Jesus Christ."

Mark grins and buzzes her again, sweeping up across the road toward the Chevy only to slam over at the last moment. Daria mouths an expletive, bug-eyed and grinning.

On his third pass, Mark reverses, coming from ahead so there is no mistake, thundering right at her. "What the hell was that!" she cries coyly, braking and leaping outside. Now Mark dives towards her, barely off the ground, bobbing and waggling his wings. Daria sprawls flat as he blasts over then cups hands to scrawl FUCK YOU in the sand, breathing hard.

High up, Mark finds an enormous orange polo shirt and drops it, Daria scuttling to snag it, then turning to brandish the garment at the plane, grinning, giggling approval. The plane buzzes off . . .

Miles on, to the snare drums, swooping harmonica and jolly trotting voices of "Sugar Pie," Daria spots Lilly Seven, bright pink beside a weathered shack under dead trees. She greets the recklessly-grinning Mark. Bold herself, she says: "Thanks for the nightie, but I don't hink I can use it." She holds it up to herself, to him.

The two wander over the desert. " — look, had a little trouble here," Mark murmurs. "Give me a life to get gas . . . "

Daria, skeptically amused: "The radio said somebody stole a plane . . . did you really steal that thing?"

"I needed to get off the ground . . . "

The Chevy rolls between bare hills, Daria driving and giggling to Mark's words, parking on a lookout. Daria reads: "Zabriskie Point . . . ancient lake beds . . . contains borates and gypsum."

"Two old prospectors" Mark mutters deadpan.

Beyond the safety wall, a violent white and gray landscape of fluffed up chemical wastes, great puffy steep hills above hammered flats, "the no-man's-land of a cataclysmic oatmeal war of pre-history."

The two drop to the slaggy ground, Mark in jeans, boots and workshirt, Daria in sandals, green-brown sensuous smock.

"Till yesterday I drove a forklift truck at a warehouse," Mark profiles. He left college for "stealing hardcover books instead of paperbacks, making phone calls on the Chancellor's stolen credit card, whistling in class . . . reprogramming the computer so it made all the engineers take art courses. It made 'em uptight!"

He asks about the strike, clumsily casual: "Oh, a cop did get killed . . . and the bushes were trampled. I was trying to find a rock station. I think they said the guy that killed the cop was white."

Mark, in a southern drawl: "Wahl, whaht man takin' up ahrms wid the blacks . . . jus' like ol John Brown!" Daria doesn't respond.

Daria screams as Mark plunges down a sheer slope, kicking up dust as he careens, backpeddling. He runs to the bottom and flops spreadeagle against the riverbed, motionless . . . then waves one hand from the wrist, feebly.

Daria follows cautiously, offers him a joint of pot.

Mark mutters: "This group I was in had rules — don't smoke. They were on a reality trip." They wander down the desolate canyon.

"Oh, yeah," Daria emotes, "they can't imagine things . . . why didn't you get out?"

"I wasn't really in the group," Mark goes on surely, speaking of the revolutionaries. Hostile: "I couldn't stand they bullshit talk . . . But when it gets down to it, you have to choose one side or the others."

Daria exults: "There's a thousand sides, not just heroes and villains."

Mark is unequivocal: "The point is, if you don't seem them as villains, you can't get rid of them."

"You think if you can get rid of them, we'll have a whole new scene?"

"Why not?"

Who's Mark's group? "You 'n me, babe!"

Daria spins and jumps, looking at the hills. It's peaceful here.

Mark, flatly: "It's dead."

Daria, high, wants to play a death game; walk from the valley ends annihilating life, one big killer finishing the other. Mark says no.

They wander down the dried out riverbed. Mark doesn't want to play games. But it was nice to come with a guy that doesn't use dope.

Daria grins: "I'm pretty tolerant."

High, her face rapt, attention dancing, she stares at the spiky desert flowers: "Pretend your thoughts are like plants — are they neat rows like a garden, wild things like ferns, weeds, vines?"

Mark, sighing: "I see sort of a jungle . . . "

Daria: "It'd be nice if they could plant thoughts in our heads . . . wonderful things like a happy childhood, really groovy parents . . .

Mark, bitterly: "And we'd forget how terrible it really was — "

Daria, excitedly: "But that's the point! Nothing's terrible!"

A longshop of the great desolate white-gray valley, two tiny figures. Daria wants to scream her head off. Both cry out.

Daria jumps, twirls, runs. Mark kicks and tumbles in the chemical drifts. Both run dustily down a great hill, the camera tilts up to a blinding sun . . .

Daria, wonderingly, flatly: "So anyway . . . so anyway . . . so anyway ought to be the name of someplace."

They wander along the chemical, bone white, brain gray. Mark,

Mark Frechette and Daria Halprin at ease in Death Valley.

doubtfully: "Would you like to go with me?"

Daria, tempted, tentative, testing: "Are you really asking?"

Mark, "If it's true, you'll answer?"

The bleak boy and pantherish girl sprawl on a slope, her finger-tips playing along his chest, hand at his neck, giggling to a soundless, self-conscious joke as he unbuttons her. She hugs him, face to his chest. Kissing, embracing, now nude, now not, her hands, eyes, mouth moving passionately over him. Again together, Mark dazily, the girl with fire, now bodies the gray of the dust. Daria's eyes shining. A shot of three other lovers thrashing in the dust, then Mark and an enraptured Daria, eyes enormous. More couples: blondes, brunettes, in twos and threes, twisting, tumbling in smocks and jeans in the dust and smoky ashes; Mark and Daria thrashing together. A guitar begins single notes, simple chords. Daria and Mark again and again, cut against more rolling, scuttling, leaping couples and threes, making delightful frightfulness across the blasted valley, to the strumming poignant guitar . . .

Mark and Daria lie resting, Mark's eyes closed, Daria thoughtful atop him. She looks around: Zabriskie Point is empty.

They climb to the lookout as a chubby midwestern couple roll up in an electric blue camper hauling a powerboat, a bulbous fish out of water. The fat, bermuda-shorted man whinnies "Build a drive-in up here. They'd make a mint!" His cloying wife: "Why don't you do it, honey bunch!" Their offspring sucks and licks an ice cream cone, travel stickers covering the view.

In a valley between two raw-earth bluffs, a shiny highway patrol car catches the young people unawares. Mark hides behind a red chemical lavatory.

"Having trouble . . . Where's your car?" grunts a porcine patrol-ler, tiny eyes glittering behind glinting sunglasses.

Daria, with bold casualness: "I left that, along with my driver's license, Bank of America card, travelers' checks, Social Security number, Birth certificate . . . "

The patroller looks her over slowly, hostile, ready to teach this luscious arrogant piece a lesson. Behind one cubicle, Mark covers the cop, squinting across the sight. Dara sees him, her eyes widen.

The patroller doesn't risk it, and Daris explodes: "Man you're really crazy! . . . Is it loaded?" Mark pours the bullets out. "Nope." Daria realizes: "The guy who killed the cop . . . "

"No . . . I wanted to, but somebody else was there . . . "

Daria cautions the bullets would make evidence. "Let's get out of here. If you put your hair up they'd never recognize you . . . "

Beside the shack, a dynamic Daria, a thoughtful Mark, and a grinning old man psychodelicize Lilly Seven: bright green stripes down her sides, red eyes leer around the propeller, THANX and

NO WORDS across identification numbers.

"They might not even think it's a plane," Mark muses. "Strange, prehistoric bird spotted with its genitals out."

Daria giggles. Is he crazy enough to take it back?

"Sure, you don't borrow someone's private plane, take it for a joyride, and never come back to express your thanks!"

"But why take it back. You could just ditch it . . . don't even have to risk — "

"Want to take risks," Mark iron voices.

He finishes a wing insignia: SHE : HE : IT. "Ain't she beautiful?"

The motor honks, chugs, roars; the plane, shimmering in the superheated air, trundles as Daria waves. Mark soars, retracts his wheels, roars off . . .

At the field, the stocky, angry owner is interviewed: "A small plane, but they don't come very cheap, I can tell you." Others buzz past like dragonflies. Face hostile: "My wife was in love with that thing . . . "

Above the clumped dark greens and dirty sand, Lilly Seven chugs along. On its side: NO WORDS.

In the Chevy, Daria turns on the casually agonized voices and loping guitar of "You Got the Silver." In a tenacious tracking shot, the camera follows her down the desert road . . .

High in the sky, Mark plunges, roaring at black upthrust crags, soars over, levels out along the railroad, going home . . .

Daria switches to a swift fiddle and voice: "I Wish I Was a Single Girl Again." Some horses run down the other side of the road, glossy brown, swiftly handsome . . .

In the airless mechanical landscape of the private airfield — white radar domes, orange wastecans — the police confer, domelights pulsing, radios crackling.

Lilly Seven chugs on against a cloudbank. Across a wing, ecstatically: NO MORE WAR . . .

A radio voice: "Just spotted him. Looks like he's coming in." The police slam doors, rev up. "KH-352, you should see this thing. It's got this psycho stuff painted all over it." A news copter roars in, as faintly, Lilly Seven is heard. The porcine owner looks on. Newsmen ready cameras. Cops in helmets and sunglasses watch silently . . .

Weaving and waggling its wings once more, Lilly Seven drops, roaring. Mark turns towards the police as they shoot out.

Except for roaring motors, it is still. Police squealers and siren roar. From overhead we see the brightly colored little plane turn and twist to and away from the jockeying cars on the black runway, towards the green lawn. Abruptly the plane is boxed in, the camera gives up, tumbling and spiraling silently to earth. The police,

**13**

frightened, excited, leap out, and in Mark's professional stance, start firing. From Mark's viewpoint: honking squealers, banging pistols. Silence. The cops approach, pistols out. Something is slumped on the instruments. Silence, They peer in. A hoarse voice: "Call an ambulance." The helicopter comes down whistling . . .

Daria stands beside her car in a copse of dark green cactus, head bent, tranced with grief. The car radio blasts: " . . . several shots were fired into the cockpit by an unidentified police officer, killing the youth immediately . . . " Daria stands and listens to the stoical guitar and harp of "Dance of Death," wavering from side to side, dark dress amid dark cactus . . .

In the pearly Chevy, a stricken-faced Daria drives across a dry brown basin scabrous with scrub, takes a crossroad, forges up a hill. In glimpses we see a wide, sundecked building atop it. constructed of desert wood and sandstone to blend with the mountain. Close up, it is a Wrightish fortress — eerie, sundecked, glasswalled, pooled, embracing the peak. Daria parks beside half a dozen powerful dreamboats.

She walks in slowly, breathing hard, to silence; then, splashing. Some confident middle-aged women in bikinis are gathered around the pool. "Nikki, you know, said she *wasn't there*, but I walked up *by mistake* . . . " Daria somnabulates into a grotto-corridor, water drooling down stone face. She stumbles off the path, into the wall's pool, pressing against the stone, weeping, gasping.

Inside, it's silent, but for faint wind chimes. A half dozen steely-faced men confer in tense tones in an enormous, frontier-decorated modern room. Daria stops before a massive black maid with a re-signed expression. The girl stares at the conference, her face ghost-like in the glass . . .

"Well, Lee, if these are your final conditions, I don't see how we can submit them to our associates. This proposal is just unacceptable," mildly exclaims a grizzled, wiry Westerner.

Smoothly: "But is this land of value to you people or not?"

"Frankly, I don't think that it is . . . "

Lee and associate confer on the terrace. "Shall we call their bluff?"

Lee sees Daria, genially: "What happened to you — try and go swimming? Go downstairs, change clothes; your room is first on — "

The girl goes wordlessly off.

On the stairs, Daria exchanges a silent smile with a young Indian servant girl. Daria's own face is strange. She emerges, to drive down the mountain in the old car in the golden light of the desert's late afternoon . . .

We see the large empty rooms of the desert house, Daria staring upwards . . .

The intent faces of the executives peer down at a model of Sunnydunes. The planned lakes are mirrored, so the determined, clever faces are reflected, wraithlike, from among the colored markers and contoured plaster of paris. Lee's voice, dimly: "Great potential . . . lends itself to casual living . . . yet it's affluent . . . "

Daria stares upward, her face impassioned, surrounded by the gold and dark green desert, confronting the lavish fortress. We see the deserted sundeck, abandoned magazines flapping . . .

Silently, the house rips apart and outward, its center a blazing orange fireball, timbers and stones and glass arching outwards, flying free!

From close, the house whole. BRAAMMGHHH! The house lets go, again the orange cloud raging outwards, black smokewreath behind, trailing skyward glass, stone, metal thrown high, timbers flapping and turning in the air —

Again, from closer, lower: BRAAMMGH! The house lets go, orange flower, crazy ebony burst in moments, then rising to a high black mushroom, tumbled fragments beginning to spill —

Again, closer, orange blast spotted with twisting, twirling bits, black cylinder rising, flattening, rupturing sundeck, flashes in the rubble, pieces thumping to earth.

Fifth time, closer, louder, shadows shifting, orange blast canted off-center, smoky column flattening, fires and smoke and tumbled ruins.

And six, closer, louder; again; again; orange balloon, black swirling envelope, climbing, flattening, shrapnel fixtures, wooden boards dancing, a dozen pyres in the ruins.

Again, roaring, flaming; and at last: very close up; blast, flameball, smoke column rising, flattening, tossed fragments, gutted ruin, flickering pyres —

Now, to electronic angelic moans, a slow guitar beat, a strange windy harp sound, more destruction: patio furniture ripples and fragments, drifting slowly upwards as it dreamily shatters in ultra-fast filming . . .

A closet of fine clothes lackadaisically breaks up, the cloth lazily tearing and twirling to the humming, whispering music, punctuated by swift, abstracted wails . . .

A television set shatters itself with infinite deliberation, bits of tubes and wires drifting about like the wastes in an unattended fishtank, the picture tube exquisitely dispersing in a shimmering, gyrating crystalline cloud; tangled circuitry weightless and tumbling lazily.

A refrigerator ruptures open, spilling a fish, sausages, a loaf of Wonder Bread, all swimming or hanging, the fish most unnaturally. Fragments of watermelons hang in a coarse dispersal.

More goods tumble and spin. *Look* magazine, Kellogg's K, globs

**15**

Daria Halprin watches, transfixed, as an elegant desert house "explodes".

of milk and juice, a can of soup, all suspended, to moans and wails and chords. At last they begin to drift downwards . . .

A bookcase joins the slow rain, volumes tumbling, pages flapping dispiritedly, torn bindings with threads and ripped sheets trailing, sail across the screen with giddy deliberateness . . .

Daria turns her back to the high citadel, black smoke and flames silently rising, timbers crackling. The pearly Chevy points forward down the road. The shot is suffused with the golden light. She gets in, starts up. The camera drfits to the rich setting sun. Soft theme up: "Dawn comes up so young. Dreams begin so young . . . Zabriskie Point is anywhere . . . "

Before **Zabriskie Point**, Antonioni's films had received considerable critical attention and praise. **L'Avventura, Il Deserto Rosso**, and **Blow-Up** were considered major works of cinema art, and Antonioni's very personal style had been analyzed into a few strong elements:

*a severe, classical cinematographic style*: Antonioni's frames were beautifully composed, real "paintings in light," carefully considered in terms of color and tone variations, balance, perspectives and framing, dominance, unities, and dissonances. The movements within each shot were carefully set up to maintain this power and effectiveness.

*description of feelings through precise images*: Antonioni rejected the use of interior monologues, "loaded" dialogue, or melodramatic music to convey his characters' feelings and relationships. Instead, he used precise images to carry moods and meanings: an image of two characters wordlessly implied one's ascendancy, distrust, or distance from the other; their movements and gestures displaying their emotional maneuverings.

*use of landscapes, fragmentary details*: His concentration on images led to using landscapes as characters. The broken-up, harsh island in **L'Avventura** reflects the arid, unsatisfactory relations between the bored characters. This tendency has been neatly summed up as "environment is destiny."

*prominence of women*: Antonioni's films are unusual for the important roles and emphasis given female characters. The director has commented he finds women more aware and responsive to the emotional subtleties of modern life.

*advanced Marxist-psychoanalytic themes*: Antonioni's later films are concerned with all the complexities and ambiguities of living in an advanced technological, capitalistic society, particularly distortions in personal character and love relationships. Because of this, the films tend towards multiple levels of signification.

*making the audience work*: Antonioni expects all his audiences to make an effort. In speaking of **L'Avventura** (2.20): "I want the audience to work. I ask them to see the film from the beginning and devote their full attention to it, treating it with the same respect they would give a painting, a symphony, or any other work of art."

All these stylistic components are clearly present in **Zabriskie Point**. Nevertheless, many previously enthusiastic critics (Pauline Kael, Stanley Kauffmann) were very displeased with the film, and tended to write it off as pretentious, cliched, and even a shameless attempt to revitalize guttering creative fires (Antonioni is 57) by mindlessly identifying with "youth."

Antonioni himself took pains to explicate these admitted limitations where they existed (1.6): "It's very easy for an American to say to me, 'You're an Italian; you don't know this country. How dare you talk about it!' But I wasn't trying to *explain* the country — a film is not a social analysis, after all. I was just trying to feel something about America, to gain some intuition. If I were an American, they would say I was taking artistic license, but because I'm a foreigner, they say I am wrong. But in some ways a foreigner's judgement may be . . . not better, necessarily, but more objective — illuminating precisely because it is a little different."

Antonioni begins with radical students, hidden in a golden, muffling glow. Seen clearly, they are not so attractive, but really, more complex and interesting — and pretty clearly don't have a chance. Cohen (1.4) notes Catherine Cleaver's self conscious smile at Antonioni's camera, a corporate eye even in the revolutionary sanctorum. Mark, instinctively rejecting all the organization and talk, walks out. Radical newspaper critics complained that the real movement had gone beyond this ambience of impotence, ineffectiveness. But out of the circling arguments and viewpoints, one key idea keeps centering: How is the white person to be radicalized?

The next sequence introduces and characterizes the three major protagonists. Mark, driving his roommate to a demo, is identified as ex-middle class, and more important, admits: "People only act when they need to — and I need to sooner than that." Mark's rebellion, triggered by the police roughing up, is wild, childish, and finally suicidal.

Daria is developed as a gorgeous, independent, apolitical head, though a searcher in books, for a book, a teacher, a lover . . . She is able to accommodate herself to the system, working when she needs the "bread," but living her own way, including "playing her abundant sensuality on the world like a searchlight." (1.3)

Finally, Lee Allen, the cool corporate executive, is shown in all his power and isolation. Some critics argue that Lee in his corporate role is typical of the film's unattractive adults, but Antonioni disagrees (1.6): "Nobody in the film is really personally unpleasant. Rod Taylor . . . is individually sympathetic but everyone is cut off from everyone else. That's the thing I was trying to show. The executives in their towers, although so powerful, are actually solving idealized problems, not the real ones, the ones in the streets below, the ones they cannot even see."

Allen's character limits and vulnerabilities are clear: he is anxious about the straying Daria, fearing a rival; his cheerful front is constantly tested; frustrated, he slumps like an ignoble Lincoln, turning on a discussion of his swelling fortunes to cheer himself up.

The section also shows the contrasting life choices available: a battered pickup truck or an air-conditioned Buick, risking your life against police lines or spending it discussing the merits of commercials with plastic people (the last an amusing comic conceit). It's noted that the designation on the University's liberal arts building has the same modern aluminum letters as the Sunnydunes Building sign — the system is everywhere.

Radical newspapers have complained that in the police shoot out, it's clear Mark doesn't fire his pistol. True, but consistent. Mark is a righteous, confused, excited young man, a prematurely radicalized bourgeois — but not ready to shoot. Antonioni comments: (1.6) "Even though a lot of young people talk about violence and revolution, not *all* of them could do it. It's not easy to be violent. Mark wanted to shoot the policeman . . . but he couldn't. In some cases violence is justified, but with many students violence is just an intellectual thing — something quite different from the violence that comes out of the conditions of life in a Black ghetto, where there are practical, material forces that push people into violence." Mark flees across the silent manicured lawns, a suggestion all his rage is the product of wild coincidences; that nearly everywhere things are quite, tidy, just.

The billboards he confronts rising from the polluted urban griddle are a continuation of the theme of layers of society jostling, distorted viewpoints in conflict: larger than life, garishly-colored aped existence, like the plastic people in the commercial or the desert chalet with fortress overtones. Paralleling this is the theme of social distrust: the arsenals of the gun stores, the pugnacious, violent police, even the storekeeper who won't trust Mark because it meant he'd "have to trust everybody in the whole world." In an unlikely break for freedom, Mark steals Lilly Seven, breaking the social codes himself.

In brief shots, Antonioni sums up his protagonists: Mark plunging upward, overpowered engine roaring wildly, exuberant, in trouble; Daria pleased, peaceful, searching in the quiet smooth old Chevy, munching an apple with Eve's bright eyes; Lee Allen mur-

muring and manipulating with shrewd business types in aircon-
ditioned offices.

Daria stops in a desert town, seeking some wisdom. But the adult
and the ancient she finds are narrowminded and awash in nostalgia —
no counsel here. And the children she encounters are far stranger
and wilder than herself (or Mark) — autistic, prematurely sexual,
apparently without adults to care for them — (there is no sign of
James Patterson). Disturbed and finally frightened, Daria flees the
symbols of past and future.

Now Mark, who has seen her at the water tank, begins exuber-
antly "buzzing" the Chevy, wildly waving his wings, a strange but
exhilarating "courtship," apparently undertaken for its own sake.
A few miles on, the two meet, testing and tantalizing each other as
they play across Zabriskie Point.

Many critics have objected to this section, finding the dialogue
painfully awkward. The material itself is adequate: Mark's prospec-
tor joke, his list of university pranks, his pessimism; Daria's games
and delight in his rebellion. But the delivery is painfully offkey and
uneven. Cohen (1.4) has shrewdly commented on this: "what is
'acting'? Convincing another that one *is* the character one is supposed to be . . . [But] how can a human being who is unconvincing
to himself — and this is precisely the dilemma of 'Mark' and of most
politically interested but uncommitted students — how can this
human being seem convincing to others? And in this 'acting' sense?
It is impossible. But it is real."

As the two drift over the bleached ground Mark's naive politics
stumblingly emerge: "A white man taking up arms with the blacks
. . . on a reality trip . . . if you don't see them as villains, you can't
get rid of them." Daria's own ideas are playful, protean: "Pretend
your thoughts are like plants . . . nothing's terrible! . . . plant good
thoughts in your head." Mark not quite asks her to go on with him,
she almost wants to agree, but the chance slips away. Antonioni
does not make them sympathetic lovers or radicalize the relationship.

Urging him on, her eyes brilliant, the two begin to make love.
The other couples that spring up on the dusty hillsides, a horizon-to-
horizon love-in, seem to be Daria's drugged hallucination, the sensual
girl's first political vision — a communal sexuality. It is clear from
the compositions that she skillfully dominates the lovemaking and
the napping Mark, her eyes staring compassionately at the wasteland
and him. Moments later this "pure" act of love is contrasted with
the pudgy self-satisfied couple and their slurping offspring, and the
rape-ready highway patroller.

Suddenly, irrationally, Mark chooses to return the stolen Lilly
Seven. Daria makes clear it's a senseless risk, but he "wants to take
risks" — or die, or assert his Quixotean nature against her. The

psychodelia on the plane are expressions of such a nature — and certain to infuriate the police. Mark gets into the plane, and we never see him again. Daria departs again smoothly, listening to rock radio, while Lilly Seven roars down the sky. Coming in, Mark waggles his wings in the same ingratiating gesture, but he is no longer in the free desert limbo, but the airless technological supercity. The squad cars, like police dogs, surround the gaily painted metal bird. Shots, and the camera, like a free spirit blasted, tumbles to earth. Youthfully, stupidly, impotently, Mark dies. That's all there is to his rebellion.

Daria hears on the radio, the youth shot by an "unidentified police officer." Her face works as she drives towards the crag house but, dry-eyed, she can only lean against the water spurting from the rocks. Sarris (1.11) argues that the characters' psychological deadness requires Antonioni to keep coming up with *visual* correlatives for their feelings of pain, entrapment (the dying camera), outrage (the exploding house), which weaken the film.

In any case, the movie has shifted, something at last has penetrated Daria's sensual, protean optimism. In meeting the old resigned-looking black maid and the young Indian one, things shift again. Cohen (1.3) suggests it's Daria's awareness that the bright-featured Indian girl will inevitably grow impassive and obedient, in spite of all her smiles. This Daria refuses to do.

The final explosions are surely one of the most devastating sequences in the film, destroying all the proudest achievements of our material civilization: the crag mansion, tentatively and then in swift determined repetitions, finally with a collage of consumer goods in strange, slow motion deliberateness — a refrigerator, food, a television, pool furniture, a case of books. But these are Daria's head explosions, for Daria has taken over the film. For the first time, she is negative and destructive.

Commenting on the final moments of the film, the director states: (1.6) "I wouldn't start a revolution by blowing up a house. The explosion of the house is not exclusively a symbolic comment; it is a clear expression of how the girl feels at that precise moment. I am telling her story, and that is why I don't end the film at that point. Instead, I show her returning to the car after the explosion."

Now tranquil and resolved, aware of her true feelings, Daria moves off through the golden romanticizing light we first saw, perhaps Antonioni's own skeptical last word on the girl. But the initial question — whence radicalization? — has been answered.

Besides commenting on **Zabriskie Point**, Antonioni has been questioned extensively on the social and political realities of America. He finds he is instinctively brought to make common cause with

America's rebelling youth, attracted by this natural animal vitality, and because "they know what the adults ignore. They know that reality is an impenetrable mystery, and it is in the nature of today's children not to succumb passively before this mystery, and not to calmly accept the adult vision of reality, which seems to have produced monstrous results." (1.1)

Antonioni, however, says he has never been concerned with the relationship of technological progress to the human mind, a problem he regards as peripheral to our real difficulties. "My interest is not in man facing machine but in man facing man, with his acts, his story, his attempts at love, according to the style, the pace, the place, and the occasions which today's civilization allow. It is not the command of the machine which is slipping away from man, but control of his sentiments, his beliefs." Antonioni would like to see machines molded and restricted to man's measure, not a ban on machine progress altogether. He confirms Callenbach's (1.3) description of his work as "a desperate rearguard defense of traditional humanism . . . against the dissolving power of the acids produced by our advanced industrial society," in this case with the almost animal magnetism of Daria Halprin.

On the possibility of a real revolution? "Perhaps in fifty years things will have evolved to a crucial point and these forces we are now feeling underneath will explode. Who's to say? . . . " Nor does Antonioni advocate revolution. But he does detect "a silent revolution going on already. The mentality of the people in this country is changing . . . In a sense, there is a violent revolution taking place too, one that is caused by things, objects which are supposed to be helping people. They do help some people, of course, but they also assault and disrupt. That is why a refrigerator behind a shop window in Watts becomes a revolutionary object. In **Zabriskie Point** I suggested that the material wealth of America, which we see in advertisements and on billboards along the road, is itself a violent influence, perhaps even the root of violence. Not because wealth is bad, but because it is being used not to solve the problems of society, but instead to try and hide these problems from society." (1.6)

# John Boorman

# POINT BLANK

**Point Blank** began for English director John Boorman when Lee Marvin and producer Judd Bernard came to him in London with a script by David and Rafe Newhouse. Boorman never managed to read the novel *The Hunter* by Richard Stark, which the first treatment was vaguely based on, but the script itself was deliberately done as a throwback, old-fashioned gangster film. Boorman was more excited about the chance to work with Marvin. He took the job.

The director then proceeded to completely re-write the script with Alexander Jacobs. Boorman knew everything he wanted, but Jacobs was particularly good as a "constructionist," making the plotting work out, and as a dialogue writer. Lee Marvin also helped.

Boorman gradually became enthused about **Point Blank**'s protagonist, and wanted to make him a truly contemporary American character. Most of his work was in building up Walker (Lee Marvin), realizing his character, predicaments, and relationships; Boorman is still dissatisfied with the last: for example the sense of comradeship with Reese, with homosexual overtones, shows incompletely in the way he manhandles an uncertain Walker at the all-male reunion, Marvin reacting like a passive girl. This idea is echoed further on, when Walker dumps Reese out of bed. Every scene, in fact, has such an echo.

Boorman always worked backwards from his archetypical American protagonist. He chose Los Angeles for the action because he felt it emblematic of Walker's own emptiness, isolation, and alienation, and the violence which it produced as the only way to release the pent-up feelings. Alexander Jacobs suggests Walker came to reflect Los Angeles in his implacable, never-let-up drive, an indisputable aspect of what America is, take it or leave it. Walker is thus typical of the Anglo-Saxon approach to visual art, which often stresses it as social observation, "highly skilled, very effective, and sketching in and drawing of a social page." (2.3)

Atonal strings, forghorns, over some dingy, mist-laden buildings . . .

Echoing gunblast! . . . A second! In a prison cell, Walker (Lee Marvin) is thrown back on the bunk, dazed, wonderingly: "Cell . . . prison cell . . . where?"

Cut to hall jammed with suited, staggering men: party sounds, tobacco haze, jeering harmonica. A sweating, hysterical man husks: "I want to talk to you, Walker . . . C'mon, *Walker!*" Bleary Walker can't hear. The other, "I *NEED YOUR HELP!*"

Shot: The two in rough jackets, workpants, wait on a grill-enclosed walkway, drab brick buildings behind. The grinning, nervous man is Mal Reese (John Vernon). "They use the prison . . . it's closed . . . we take it from them . . . (pleading), you're my friend . . . I can't make it on my own . . . "

Walker's voice, muzzily, "Help my friend — "

At the party, Pleader Reese knocks Walker down. On the floor, he grabs him, surrounded by feet: "Help me, help me — "

Same walkway, at once it's night. A helicopter roars in.

On the same floor, Reese screaming: "I owe a bundle! . . . They're gonna kill me!" The copter roars down into the prison courtyard.

On the floor: "We just knock 'em on the head and that's it!"

Two men exchange packages with the pilot in the brick courtyard, trot up towards the walkway.

Walker and Reese leap out, Reese shooting the men as they scream, Walker shouting. Reese: "We made it!" Walker, sour: "We blew it!" A lovely blonde girl in a jumpsuit joins them.

In a cellblock, she counts the money — $93,000. "Darling!" she husks to Reese.

Reese, flatly: "You'd better take care of your husband."

In a cell, Walker slumps, the girl (Sharon Acker) beside him.

"Lynn, c'mere," husks Reese at the door. As the girl comes out, he clutches her and shoots the prone, helpless Walker. ECHOING GUNBLAST! . . . A second!

The girl jerks, screams, face in his coat: "Take me away!"

Walker looks up: empty dark red, gray, black cells, falling rows of sunlight. "A dream, a dream — " he murmurs vaguely.

To drifting horns, in compositions against grills, rusted grates, broken glass, knotted barbed wire lit with tainted sunlight, Walker staggers through abandoned Alcatraz. For moments he hangs on a fence against the sky, seagulls and clouds wheeling. At last, he stumbles into the bay, and in a stiff-armed crawl swims towards the San Francisco skyline . . .

Shots of a concrete island bastion.

A professionally sweet voice, badly amplified: "This, then, is

Alcatraz, the treacherous currents around the island rendering it virtually escape proof . . . "

Walker, impassive in a business suit, stands on the excursion boat's deck as it rounds the prison island . . .

The girl lists the few, unsuccessful escape attempts.

A tough voice: "How did *you* make it, Walker?" A heavy, bald, ironic man in his forties stands behind the doublecrossed thief. They go inside the cabin.

"I'm Yost . . . " says the man (Keenan Wynn). "I want the Organization . . . your friend Reese . . . he's in the bigtime now — suits, penthouses. . . He bought his way back in with the money he stole from you." "93,000 . . . you want Reese . . . and I want the Organization." Yost has a piece of paper: "I'm gonna help ya . . . that's your wife's address in Los Angeles . . . Reese lives there, too."

Feet banging remorselessly on the tiles, face immobile, Walker pounds through the Los Angeles Air Terminal. The implacable noise continues to shots of: the lovely Lynn rising from a luxurious bed, scanning a long line of dresses; Walker marching on; Lynne applying eye makeup; Walker driving through Los Angeles; Lynne regarding herself in a beauty salon's infinite regression of mirrors; Walker slumping at the wheel watching her go into her apartment . . .

She turns to lock up — Walker smashes in! Enormous pistol raised, knocking her dizzy, seizing her, dragging her, legs bunched below mini-skirt, kicking doors open to the bedroom to blast half a dozen great holes in the mattress. In the bathroom, he hits colored glass vials of bath oils, perfumes, shampoos to the floor in a psychedelic swirl . . .

Silent, Walker slumps on the couch. Head drooping, Lynne mutters brokenly: "Walker, Reese isn't here . . . he's gone, three months ago, gone, cold, moved out . . . Walker, I'm glad you're not dead . . . you ought to kill me . . . Guy brings the money first of every month . . . just couldn't make it with you . . . with him it was — kind of fun . . . that night on Alcatraz . . . I knew it was you I really wanted . . .

She gets up, wanders, to dreamy organ, notes: "Do you remember how we met . . . the rain . . . "

On a misty dock, Lynne in a white shift, hair bound, mouth tight, Walker in rough clothes in casual pursuit, grinning.

Lynne, dreamy-husky: "You were a little drunk . . . so was I . . . you were funny when you were drunk . . . "

The two face, smiling shyly, she lets down her hair. In a cut, in swimsuits, they dive into a wave, laughing —

"It was wonderful at first . . . I loved you . . . then Mal happened — "

Mal at the reunion, waving, shouting, grinning wildly. The three in the front seat of a car, images of trees sliding up the windshield. Lynne leans on Walker, puts on his sunglasses, then sits in the middle with a little smile — and starts to lean in the other direction, towards Mal.

"I was happier then than at any other time . . . suddenly I began to drift towards Mal . . . and I . . . I just went with it."

Abruptly, the living room, the two sitting and staring, silent.

Lynne goes into the bedroom while Walker lies on the couch as it grows darker . . .

In slow motion, to eerie whistling: in the cell block, Mal twists her away, fires; Walker smashes in, snagging her, lurching on . . .

Walker tumbles off, sprawling awake. Lynne, dressed, is on the bed, an empty pill bottle on the night table. Her long hair drapes to the floor. Walker holds her, pushes his wedding band on her finger next to her own . . .

In daylight, a zombie Walker peers blearily between the drapes, out the window. The focus sharpens . . . outside, Yost nods . . . Now in the bathroom, music eerie, Walker sends more bottles crashing. In the bedroom, suddenly unfurnished, he sits drawn up, features blank. Again he recalls the betrayal.

A mild young boy with an envelope bangs on the door, and is yanked in and spreadeagled. Faintly: "I got a call." Walker, patiently: "You got a call."

"They'll kill me." "They'll kill you . . . "

"Big John Stegman, Big John's Car Lot." . . .

Below a Big John sign, cars are lined up in bright platoons, chrome winking. A smiling, smug, fortyish man with a thin mustache watches his young salesman smooth-talking a blonde against a racy Corvette.

Walker appears, deadfaced. Courteously: "Mr. Stegman?"

In a mock coy voice, innocently: "Yes sir, that's me!"

Walker wants a car, maybe this one. Mal Reese sent him. Stegman offers a spin, eyes on the blonde. Walker buckles his seatbelt: "Most accidents happen within three miles of home."

Walker wheels it out, while Stegman tunes his commercial on the stereo.

"I like the power steering myself!" Walker yells, flying towards a cement truck only to dodge it at the last moment. "You're crazy!" Stegman yelps.

To hornblasts, squeals of brakes and tires, Walker plunges down the street. "What're ya doin' to my car?" "What I did to your delivery boy! Where's Reese?"

The car squeals round a corner at full speed. Stegman: "I can't tell ya!"

With a crash Walker penetrates a metal mesh fence. He rams a massive concrete freeway support, the car's metal screaming.

A bloody, bruised Stegman wails: "Stop it, stop it!"

"I want Reese!"

Walker slams engine and trunk into the pillars, smashing both. He rams the front once more, shoots backwards so the trunk collapses. Metal screams and bangs, Stegman yelps, the radio plays tinnily; Stegman stabs: "I know about you, Walker! How's your wife!"

"She's dead!"

The wheels scream, the frame bangs, the fenders and hood spring loose. "How does that grab ya, Stegman?" Walker throws him from the wreck.

Walker, deadly soft: "Where's Reese?"

"Lynne's sister runs a trap. A place called the Loony House." Stegman keeps trying to close the hopelessly sprung and out of shape door. The car is a junkyard heap. The radio prattles: "You'll love my guarantees, you'll love my cars, you'll love Big John!"

On a green hill, Walker looks down at Lynne's grave, face calm. He strides off. Behind him, a yellow mechanical grab revs up. clawing out more graves, squeaking . . .

Big John faces Reese across the wrecked car under the lot's nightlights. It is a broken twisted wreck, the red undercoat to the white paint visible in streaks. "Did I exaggerate?"

"I didn't tell him anything — " There's a bandaid across his nose, a blood bruise on the dapper salesman's forehead.

"Why didn't he kill you?"

"He killed the car!" . . .

"Just don't hold out on me," Reese mutters. "Find him . . . just do it!" . . .

An enormous mouth, in a wailing yelp: YAH–HUH, *YAHHH–*HUHHHH . . . " It is a screaming black entertainer on a stage, in a dark, close, hot place where electric music thrums. "YAHHH . . . *YAH*–HUH . . . " The black runs back and forth as Walker slouches at a table in the murk, getting Chris's address from a waitress friend. The black keeps going "YAH–HUH . . . YA–HA–HA–ha–ha–ha."

Onstage, screens flash with a lightshow: color patterns, Victorian pornography, belly dancers. The crowd pumps approval.

The black crouches on one knee, extending the mike to a fat, red-necked, curly-headed harmonizer: "YAH–HUH?" "*AH*–HUH! *YAH*–YAH . . . YA–YA–ya–ya . . . "

To thrumming and screamed yelps Walker tries to lose his tails, going back of the stage. A girl in a bikini struts and prances: images of writhing legs, 18th century debauch, abstract prisms glow on her . . .

A dark shape springs! Walker smashes it back into a rack of

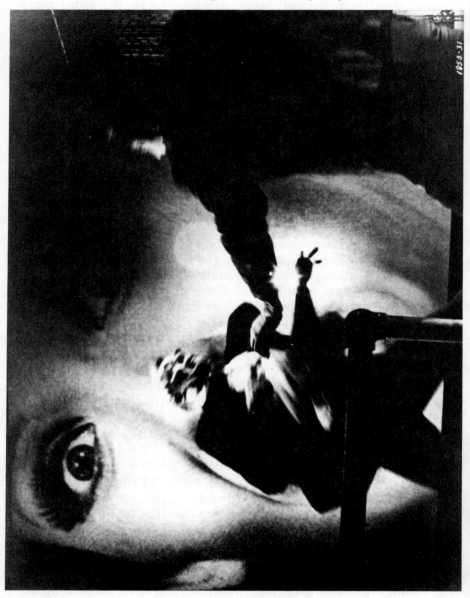

Walker (Lee Marvin) slugs his way out of the "Looney House" nightclub, as Botticelli and Rubens nudes flash on the screen.

silvery film cans which bursts, raining down. The music pounds, black and white yelp, another attacker flings himself! Walker rabbit-punches him to a table, locks fists together, whips full around, a pitiless hammer to the man's groin so he spasms, screaming. Above the slugfest, alternate images: a girl's face screaming in horror, crying out ecstatically. A real go-go girl screams harshly at the bloody twitching muggers.

The black and "Curly" wail and yelp, music strumps, a lightshow image of a woman flaps a moment on Walker's impassive face . . .

Walker slips towards a dark, comfortable hillside home, gun out. On the sleeping loft, a bedlamp illuminates a sprawled figure, a very attractive exhausted young woman, much resembling Lynne. The gunman hunches, knocks a pilljar from the night table. She gasps huskily: "Walker!" He tells her Lynne is dead.

"I hear you're runnin' with Reese."

Chris (Angie Dickinson) sourly: "Well, you heard wrong . . . he makes my flesh crawl . . . "

Walker wants him. "He owes me money."

Chris lies in bed, blanket back, hair tousled, studying him: "Lynne and money . . . I got an extra room, you can stay here if you want."

"We'll get him!"

Reese, well dressed, enters a great modern business slab. A secretary signals admission to a second office, he is frisked politely, and finally allowed inside.

In an executive suite, Carter, a suave type, studies him coolly: "What the hell're you fooling around with now, Reese — you're trouble. Wherever you go, trouble finds you out." Carter takes his own pills. "What's the story?"

"The Alcatraz run . . . he was with me. I needed all of it to pay you back."

"You left with Walker's share, and his wife."

"He killed her."

Carter hesitates: "Tell you what, we'll let him follow you." . . .

Chris and Walker cruise a city street in her Sunbeam. They pass the Huntley, a massive ebony black and snowy white hotel. An external elevator slowly slides up to the penthouse.

Walker: "What's it like?"

"Fort Knox."

Husky silent men stand by the entrances and ramp. A squad of airline stewardesses click-clack leggily out. Walker notes a residential apartment house opposite the syndicate citadel . . .

On the palm treed boardwalk, Walker quizzes Chris as he jerks a telescope around to study the Huntley. Chris, moodily: "You'll have trouble getting in, but you'll never get out."

"How bad does he want you, Chris?"

"Oh, (shrugs), I don't know, who knows . . . pretty bad, I guess."

"Bad enough to let you through?" . . .

In the plush lobby, Chris strides to the elevator, ignored by the hardguys. "This way to heaven," one mocks.

The elevator moves smoothly up the building's night face, Chris staring at the lights below. She comes out past a relaxed, talkative phalanx of toughs. Shyly, to a pullovered, glittereyed figure: "Lo, Mal."

Across the street, in a shabby dried-flowers and doilies apartment, Walker tells the effeminate owners to tie themselves up. They apologetically comply.

High above, Mal: "Well, Cinderella . . . "

"It's a woman's privilege to change her mind . . . all good things come to those who wait."

"Then I won first prize . . . Scotch? . . . You know how long I been hung up on you? Since the first time I saw you . . . and Lynne."

Out of his sight, her face twists . . .

Deadpan, Walker calls the cops and holds the phone to his host; who squeals: "Help me, please . . . I'm being attacked . . . Ferguson, . . . 2291 Western — "

Upstairs, Mal unbuttons Chris' blouse, pulling back the sheet. She embraces him, his eyes haunted.

Downstairs, as police sirens wail, Walker strides down the garage ramp . . .

In the penthouse, the hardguys calm an excited Mal. Chris in her robe pulls the bedroom curtains, seizes him desperately, pulls him down.

On the penthouse balcony, Walker has gagged and tied the guards and tilted their bodies over the rail in a degrading, helpless posture. He dumps the pistols down the drain, rattling.

Mal and Chris are on the big bed, clutching, as Walker ducks in. Chris looks toward him over Reese's shoulder, agonized. Walker suddenly wrenches him off the girl, jams the gun in his face: "I want you to come with *me*, Mal. I want my $93,000!"

Chris scampers away, dresses in the shadows.

Mal is shivering, terrified. With grotesque modesty he hugs the sheet. "You don't stand a chance," he manages, then faints.

Walker slaps him. "Wake up, Mal!" In a sincere whisper: "Let's go!"

"Let me go, Christ!"

"Oh, no, I want you *this* way, Mal." Walker tries to question the frightened man, tumbling him over, gun at his throat: "Names, Mal, names!"

"Fairfax . . . Brewster . . . Carter!" Mal gasps. "C'mon, kill me, c'mon!"

"Who do you work for?"

"Carter . . . *It won't do you any good! . . .* Steward Building . . . it's called — the Multiplex Company . . . twelfth floor — " Walker forces him to his feet, towards the rooftop.

"I'll get it for you! Trust me, Walker!"

Flash to the reunion, Walker and Mal in the feet forest, Mal shouting: "Trust me, Walker, you're my last chance!"

Walker hustles him out: "We'll do this one together, Mal!"

On the dark, windy, flat rooftop, Mal struggles with Walker, caught in the sheet. An organ note rises eerily. Suddenly he twists free, over the edge, naked, arms outstretched, pinwheeling down, hits, is crushed by a passing car.

A crowd forms instantly, police whistles screeching.

The excited hardguys run to it, are waved back.

Walker stalks through the echoing garage. A hardguy sees him from the ramp and begins firing excitedly. Walker steps behind a pillar, a wailing cruiser slams up behind the enforcer, a cop shoots him disablingly, he's manhandled away, shouting in agony, hopping.

Walker drifts through the gabbling crowd as an ambulance screeches up. A pimply teenager stares and stares. Shouts, confusion. A stolid Yost sees them cover the face, load Mal into the meat wagon, wail off.

Walker finds a still shocked Chris nearby: "Yeah, he fell . . . "

Bitterly: "You should've killed 'im, you owed it to yourself . . . you died on Alcatraz, all right . . . G'bye, Walker."

Walker into a streetphone: "I'd like the number of the Multiplex Products Company . . . "

At a crowded, name-button business convention, Walker shuffles behind a genial Carter. "Mr. Carter, I want something . . . my $93,000 . . . "

To his arguments: "It's your problem now. Reese is dead . . . they scraped his body up off the sidewalk in front of the Huntley."

A young woman smiles at them, murmurs: "Don't monopolize him" to Carter.

"Then his debt died with him," Carter smiles sickly.

"Wrong . . . it's passed on to you."

"No corporation in the world would recognize a debt of that kind."

Flatly: "I want my money in twelve hours. I'll pick the drop. If you don't, you are dead." . . .

The smiling businessmen push past them. An American flag hangs in the background . . .

In his executive suite, Carter, mask off, rages to the lined-up hardguys: "I said nobody was to go up there! He could have done

31

Walker (Lee Marvin) examines the dead Carter (Lloyd Bochner), his credit cards forming a ribbon of honor.

without a girl for one night!"

"But he told us to let her through," one whines.

Stegman, still bandaged, mutters something. Carter turns on him, "Trojan horse," Stegman smiles. "She was the Trojan horse." "You're a smart boy, Stegman," Carter snorts. He dismisses the rest, gets a brown paper package. "Profit is the only principle – you're going to pay Walker off."

Outside in blazing sunlight, Walker watches Stegman leave the slab, hidden behind a modernistic grill, then crosses to the Stewart Building.

The door to the lush Multiplex Corporation offices opens, and Walker slips inside, immediately leaning close to the receptionist, whispering intently into her ear while he kicks loose the phone jack. Done, his words make her blanch and moan, he buzzes his own way into the shakedown room, slugs the frisker-guard, plunges into Carter's executive suite. "What're you doing in here!" Carter quacks.

Walker, angry, "I want my money!" He slams Carter back against his pretty Venetian blinds so they flex wildly.

"You're crazy Walker, how can this help you!" . . .

"Let's go!" Walker hustles him down a black feeder tunnel. "I assure you, I always – "

"C'mon!"

The drainage canal is a block wide, gray concrete riverbed with high, gently sloping walls. A small stream flows down the center where Stegman stares at the furious sun.

At the mouth of the feeder, Carter, hysterical: "I'm a businessman, a man of my word, there's Stegman with your money. Get it!"

"You get it!" snarls Walker, shoving him down the slope, into the light.

Carter throws up his hands, screams: "No, it's all right!"

On a distant bridge, a rifleman blasts the darksuited Carter so he slides to the channel floor. A terrified Stegman sprints up the far wall, is shot, slides down. On the bridge, the rifleman meticulously packs his weapon, drives off after ripping up a parking ticket.

Walker waits, examines the dead. Carter's wallet holds only credit cards. Walker lets them drop, the pocketed plastic strip across the executive's chest like a ribbon of honor. He finds an address book, keeps it. The payoff package is full of blank paper. Walker kicks it into the little blue swiftflowing stream, watches it drift away . . .

Walker hands the address book and a long rifle shell to the bald, silent Yost. A big ranch estate spreads out behind them against low green hills.

Yost, rustily: "Brewster's got a meeting tomorrow morning."

Walker, flatly: "I want him alone."

**Walker (Lee Marvin) struggles with a hysterical Chris (Angie Dickinson).**

"Take it easy. You'll last longer — " . . .

To atonal bloops and tinkles in the Los Angeles night, Walker drives to Chris's ravaged home. "So they got to you . . . "

"I got well paid for fingering Reese," she says peering into a smashed mirror. Personal stuff is heaped and smashed on the floor: clothes, paintings, books. Walker picks up a flattened, twisted trumpet. "This guy you were goin' around with . . . he spent some time here, huh?"

"What about you? Are you asking me out?" . . .

In a hamburger place, the outlaw couple sit quietly together, Chris smiling at him. By contrast, two callow, not-too-bright teenagers dopily hold hands . . .

At the ranch, Walker slides the glass doors. "Brewster's, belongs to the organization . . . "

The girl looks the place over. 'I'm waiting for him . . . I thought you'd be safer with me than by yourself . . . " Walker rumbles.

Ironically: "You'll ask him for the money, he'll say no, you'll kill him."

"Yeah, somethin' like that." Annoyed: "What'd ya think this was, a pitch?"

She turns on him, angered. "Forget it!"

"You forget it!" She begins slapping and punching him, grunting, gasping, down on her knees from the effort. Walker stands rigid, silent, unmoved . . .

In the wood paneled den the gunman, blankfaced, watches TV: commercials, "sophisticated" soap opera (Junior: "You figure this'll get me over my neurotic inertia or something"), animated cartoons, commercials . . .

Sounds: a mechanical churning, roaring, buzzing . . .

In the kitchen the toaster is smoking, the mixer is churning with an empty, banging bowl, the coffee-maker is chuckling futilely, the stove blasting heat . . . Walker turns them off. Now the hi-fi blasts, the pool lights announce the ambush. Walker strides past a drunkenly dancing Chris to fumble with the tape deck switches, goes outside to darken the pool . . .

Eerie in the darkness the loudspeakers husk: "You're a pathetic sight, Walker. Chasing shadows . . . you're played out . . . it's over . . . you're finished . . . what would you do with the money if you got it? . . . It wasn't yours in the first place . . . Why don't you just . . . lie down . . . and die . . . " Inside, he finds her sprawled across the pooltable, turns, and she slugs him with the cue. Walker staggers and slides in the brightly lit room, grabs at her . . .

In bed, he kisses Chris. Rolling, arms around him, Chris becomes the tormented Lynne. Turning again, Lynne now embraces the treacherous Reese . . . Chris and Walker are still embracing on the poolroom floor . . .

Now really in bed, Chris smiles happily upwards, Walker's blocky features remorseless even in sleep . . .

In the dawnlight Chris sleeps, Walker slips on pants, scoops up gun, sidles out. Easing back the curtains for a look, there is a flash image of dead Lynne's drapes as he shifted them. Squatting to wake Chris, he flashes on the sprawled out, overdosed Lynne, hair drooping to the ground . . .

A snappy private plane races its engine, taxies to a stop. The rifleman, holding a pipe, approaches as a fat, balding, curly-headed fellow squeezes cheerily out: Brewster.

Brewster: "What do you want? — and who killed Carter?"

The enforcer: "My money . . . I did."

Brewster, with amused irony: "Oh, you did? What happened?"

The enforcer, drily: "Carter set it up. He was sure Walker should have been . . . You don't care, do you?"

Brewster, sarcastically: "No, I *love* it. That leaves you in a spot, though. You killed the man who was supposed to pay ya!"

Over the roar of the motors, the rifler mentions Walker. Brewster'll take care of Walker, he announces.

The rifleman grins: "Never happen. He's a pro. Walker's beautiful, he's tearing you apart. I'll wait for Fairfax — he'll pay me."

Brewster smiles: "And if he doesn't, you can kill him too!" . . .

Walker stares at the satin sheets, recalling the sprawled Lynne. Chris walks in wearing a short white skirt, belting it up. Coyly: "Hey . . . what's my last name?"

Walker, flatly: "What's my first name?" . . .

At the ranch entrance, Brewster stares at the hillside, whining: "Nobody did any watering! You tell people to do things around here and it doesn't make any difference . . . "

He trots towards the low ranch buildings, the chauffeur trailing with his bags. Inside, they single-file on. Walker leaps out suddenly, smashing the servant down with his pistol. Flash: the groinsmashed heavy screaming in agony. Ahead, Brewster stops dead: "Walker!"

He turns and gibbers: "You're a very bad man, Walker, a very destructive man, why do you run around doing things like this? What do you want?"

Again, flat out: "I want my ninety-three grand . . . I want my money!"

Flash: Walker with a hysterical sheeted Mal: "I want my money!"

Brewster gabbles: "Well, I'm not going to give you any money, and nobody else is either, don't you understand that!"

Flashes: Carter, frantic in the storm drain, shot, collapsing. "What about Fairfax? Will he pay me?"

36

"Fairfax is dead, he just doesn't know it yet . . . "

Walker shrugs in annoyance: "*Somebody's* gotta pay . . . " he gestures to the desk: "Make a phone call."

"Walker, it's a *waste* of *time*," a jittery Brewster whines. "You think I can go to some hole in the wall . . . you should know something about corporations. (He waves his attache case, lights a cigar) . . . we *never* see cash . . . I've got about $11 in my pocket."

Walker slumps on the couch with his pistol, as the little executive anxiously dials Fairfax. "I got a man named Walker with me . . . says we owe him $93,000."

"Are you gonna say anything?"

The loudspeaker shrugs: "Well, what d'ya want me to say?"

"He says he's going to shoot me unless I give him $93,000."

Blandly: "Threatening phone calls don't impress me."

Brewster clutches the receiver: "It looks like he's getting ready to fire the gun." But Walker blasts the loudspeaker phone itself.

Chris bursts in, absurdly apologetic: "I'm with him!"

Brewster shudders: "Oh . . . ah . . . it occurred to me that we might be able to do something for you, might even get you the money. There 's still one setup where large sums of money change hands. It's up in San Francisco . . . "

The shadowy abandoned tiers of Alcatraz. Walker high up.

Brewster, legs spread, calls up from the yard: "There's supposed to be a light on that landing. Turn it on!"

Walker closes a switch. With a loud buzz, and the open space is illuminated: "Just stay in the light," he calls down. "Nothing's gonna happen, is it?" His voice echoes.

"Just what I said was going to happen," yells Brewster in irritated tones. "The whole thing's just routine. What're you looking for, Walker?"

The prison is abruptly silent. Brewster shuffles, turning to face all the decks of cells, dark, deserted: "Walker?"

The copter buzzes overhead.

"Walker?" Brewster crows: "Coming in . . . safe as a church . . . your money!"

The sound drops, the copter hovering like an immense green glossy dragonfly. Brewster takes the box and the machine surges upwards. Silence returns in the dim, drab courtyard.

"What about Fairfax?" calls Walker.

Brewster, annoyed: "Fairfax is dead . . . or he will be tomorrow — "

"It is tomorrow — "

Walker stands in the shadows, his face dark, the light control buzzing.

Brewster grins: "Well, here's your money — " BANG!

He grunts, collapses, stretches to touch the box. "Walker, Walker," he groans.

Out of the darkness in a camel's hair coat strides a bald, stolid, rusty-voiced man: Fairfax/Yost. "Walker didn't shoot ya."

Brewster moans upward: "This is Fairfax, Walker . . . kill him!"

"You shoulda stayed an accountant!" Fairfax/Yost grunts contemptuously. Upwards: "Our deal's done, Walker! Brewster was the last one . . . thought he could take over from me!"

Silence.

Fairfax/Yost, almost enthusiastic, calls up into the darkness: "Hey, Walker — come on in with me . . . I been lookin' years for someone like you . . . Well, *come and get your money! Come and get it!*"

Walker, silent, drops back into the shadows, so he's nearly invisible.

Fairfax/Yost, yelling: *"I pay my debts! . . .* Walker? . . . Walker?"

The rifleman comes out of the shadows, nudges Brewster with his foot.

Walker fades further into the darkness.

"Well? . . . "

*"Walker? This is the last time!* How do you like that?"

The rifleman reaches for the package: "I like it!"

"Leave it!" grunts Fairfax/Yost. The two of them leave.

The money and Brewster lie floodlit in the deserted brick yard.

The camera slowly withdraws, tilts up to the San Francisco dawn skyline.

It frames a blinking navigation light on another island.

Credits.

Though **Point Blank** is a fresh, almost revolutionary approach to the thriller, certain themes and ideas in it are presaged in Boorman's only previous film, **Catch Us If You Can** (1965), an exploitation film about the Dave Clark Five that is interesting in spite of itself. The model heroine (Barbara Ferris) and her stunt-man friend (Dave Clark) try to outwit another power-oriented organization (an ad agency whose campaign uses Ferris) and reach a little island which symbolizes escape. But the agency men are already waiting, and efficiently "repossess" Ferris once more, giving the film the same sort of circular structure as **Point Blank**. The young people's flight is even turned to account by the agency flacks who explain it away as a publicity stunt, subverting any meaning it might have had as a challenge to authority. A third idea in common is the enigmatic agency head, who keeps appearing along their trail like some sort of mythic creature, finally reversing an apparent victory. An air of deception, paranoia and webworks of power is clear in both films.

**Point Blank** does rise above the first film in subtlety and comment, particularly stylistically. The first sequences, of Walker's desperate escape from Alcatraz, filled with splinters of his meeting with Reese and murderous betrayal, synthesize the best elements of post-Marienbad technique: the dazed broken isolated figure sprawled in a bizarre decaying, deserted cellblock, his mind adrift through fragmented violent memories, then the weirdly beautiful shots of the silent manshape staggering through dusty slanted columns of sunlight, over framing grills, past smashed glass, snarled barbed wire, delicately rusting green hardware; hanging halfway up the sky on a mesh fence; thrusting himself into the bay. The girl on the boat says escape from Alcatraz is impossible, and when Fairfax/Yost asks how he did it, critic Martin (2.5) can suggest perhaps he did not: "[the first unworldly sequence combined with] the long walk down the corridor of the Los Angeles Airport brings to mind visions of Orpheus emerging from Hades . . . most important, he is never directly responsible for any of the details — deaths which occur . . . **Point Blank** is just as plausible if Walker is seen as . . . a revived restless spirit, an exterminating angel returned to the living to stalk his betrayers and revenge his own death." The film can also be seen as the feverish thoughts of the dying Walker on the island: trapped in a labyrinth of past, present and future; memories, half-awareness, dreams of retribution. Both interpretations mesh with the plot. At the close, Walker, back on Alcatraz, ignores his earthly plunder, and retreats into darkness.

Though the incidents in Walker's quest can doubtless be given a mythic or totally subjective infrastructure, they are sharpest, most entertaining (even hilarious) as social comment. Scriptwriter Alexander Walker worked on the basis that television owned the ordinary adventure — **Asphalt Jungle, Harper, Sweet Smell of Success** — and had scraped those ideas bare. "We wanted to do something completely fresh. We wanted to make a film that was half-a-reel ahead of the audience" (2.3). Aesthetically **Point Blank** is outrageous, an avant-garde shoot'em-up, bypassing characterization and scene building, combining casual bloodless holocaust, New Wave visual style, inhuman driving intensity, and a depiction of society as total corruption.

In Walker's confrontation with the betraying Lynne, his suppressed fury is clear in his violent entrance and mindless blasting of the bed, as if it didn't matter *who* was in it, just what it represented must be annihilated. Beyond that the indomitable figure is silent, unmoving, hearing her out, evidencing neither rage, forgiveness, or any other emotion. For the only time in the film, recalling their meeting, he smiles. Otherwise he is blocked, and indicates no interest in Reese or the money until she dies. After a short withdrawal, he emerges obsessed by "social justice."

The one-man demolition derby with Stegman's Chrysler sets the shocking, hilarious, basically ironic tone of the rest of the film. Big John is connected somehow with the Organization, but confused with this he is the archetypical businessman-as-a-crook, the tricky, pushy, smiling-sneering car salesman ready to peddle any overpriced tailfinned hulk loaded with junky accessories, outrageous time payments, defects, planned obsolescence. As Walker demolishes the car, Stegman's own facade is broken down: he cries for mercy and taunts Walker about his wife. Indeed, the protagonist is revenging anyone who ever got suckered into a dirty deal by a smooth huckster. Walker smashes it against a freeway piling, as if he'd smash that too if he could, giving the scene the exhilarating freedom of King Kong tearing down the El. "Big John" is left listening to his own lies: "You'll love my cars, you'll love Big John!"

The scene at the Looney House is notable for its raw brutality, probably the most naked in the film. But again something paradoxical is made of it. Martin (2.5) sees the duet of the Sammy-Davis-type and the red-necked barfly as cruelly ironic: the probably bigoted man is being mocked and degraded, made into a Stepin Fetchit if only momentarily, and tricked into enjoying it. This idea seems implied again in the murderous fight backstage. Over the battle, the screens show a woman alternately screaming in horror, and crying out in ecstasy — the fact is, the moviemakers are quite aware of what they are doing, of what appeals to film audiences.

In Chris's bedroom, Walker remains wary and distrusting, the atmosphere sexless. The two make a bloodless alliance for Reese's blood: Walker for his money, Chris for her sister. Here Walker's obsession begins to take the barest comic taint: a Keatonesque stone-faced obsessive, all he can say, over and over, is: "I want my money."

This is followed by a bitterly satiric first scene in "The Multiplex Products Company" executive offices. The modern version of the Mafia has no touch of the Mediterranean. High offices in a concrete slab, attractive secretaries, clacking business machines, luxurious executive suites (and later elegant homes), smiling blue-eyed WASP personnel, all are identical with the accoutrements of any giant "up-and-up" American corporation. Boorman deliberately sought to confuse the two: "Big John" Stegman, advertised auto dealer, also handles payoffs and is an "enforcer"; our Mr. Carter has the hauteur, no-nonsense attitude and tranquilizers of a high level executive, and is an apparent pillar of the community. One is never clear, it's cynically suggested, where legitimate society leaves off and the jungle remains — or if there is any really legitimate society at all. Carter dresses down Reese like a 20-year man giving it to an executive trainee, and "payoff," "drops," and "deathtrap" slide off his tongue like some new jargon used to describe conglomerates.

This note of duplicity is sounded again as Walker cases the Huntley (another WASP name!), apparently a luxurious hotel but in truth an Organization citadel. Mocking the possibility of such single assaults, Chris' "Fort Knox" suggests Walker's cinematic relation, James Bond. In one of the few hints of character (almost the whole film is set up for shock and impact — "pointblank"), Chris allows herself to be used as sexy bait to get Reese off guard, "giving herself" to Walker's obsession. The idea is accepted easily for moral and emotional inhibitions seem non-existent except as thin facades. Walker's use of the homosexual couple as a diversion has the same efficient disinterest as everything else he does — (imagine what Scarface would've done to the two gays!). He separates Chris and Mal, apparently in the midst of intercourse, without a second thought, to ask his own murderer and the seducer of his wife for the money. His obsession has flowered into psychopathy, and from now on the confrontation scenes all echo this one: a "normal" corrupt weakling's "Trust me!" and Walker's crazed deadvoiced: "I want my money!" Yet Walker doesn't really kill *anyone* — their deaths are the products of their revealed treacherousness — Carter, Brewster, Stegman, or the panic (Reese) or the despair (Lynne) it generates, recalling the mythic interpretation. Down in the street, a repelled Chris tells him: "You died on Alcatraz, all right."

The scenes at the business convention and the Multiplex Products offices reiterate Walker's monomania and Carter's corporate personna. Carter, a high-level executive "chairman," is shown a professional hypocrite under terrific strain. His role traps him: he must support Reese, the stupid doublecrosser, against the professional Walker, admired by all; worse, he's come to think of himself as a shrewd businessman/criminal ("Profit is the only principle") and can't believe that Walker is capable of assaulting his own offices and thrusting Carter into his own deathtrap. The actual slaughter in the storm drain is an excellently shot set-piece, with the businesslike calm of Carter and then Stegman exploding into frenzied terror, too late.

The enigmatic Fairfax and Walker meet briefly, the bald man setting up the obsessed one's rendezvous with Brewster (Brewster, Fairfax and Carter are in passing all heroic names in American history!). The brief scene recalls Fairfax hovering around the first two deaths, and suggests the "deal" offered on the excursion boat was agreed to. But nothing is explicit.

The interlude in the drive-in is low key, preparation for the driving concluding minutes, but the vague pair of affectionate teenagers add, for Ross (2.6), more commentary: "they are there to allow us to take the measure of an alternative innocent state, one which is shown to be unspeakably fatuous. This Adam and Eve are vulgar, square, besotted in illusion. One cannot imagine anyone in the audience not finding the outlaw couple infinitely preferable." Boorman must be complimented on a strong stroke against America's highest current shiboleth.

At Brewster's ranch, Chris reacts violently to Walker's half-contemptuous rejection (and perhaps his passionless killing), beating away at him with her fists till she goes to her knees, then switching to a vaguely McLuhanesque (and femininity-asserting) assault using the home's appliances, at last going for his drive while he stands in the dark, husking fears and doubts from the loudspeakers like a conventional character's conscience. To all this he responds with a wooden indifference; it takes a head blow to break his psychotic-like rigidity. In a flash, Chris is linked to Lynne, Lynne to Reese, sex to betrayal. Then the couple are really in bed. But next morning, Walker reasserts the tenuousness of the connection.

Brewster's appearance displays his own cockiness, and prepares for the conclusion by bringing up both Yost/Fairfax and the rifleman. The ambush is neatly done: the slugging of the chauffeur reverberating with a flash of that lethal judo chop backstage; Brewster's frightened refusal cuing an instant's recall of the blasted, collapsing Carter. But Brewster's glib wordiness takes Walker aback, stunningly, he doubts his own monomania: "Somebody's gotta pay," he mumbles. For a stunning instant, Walker seems an incredibly lucky moron. The scene shifts; Walker is clearly playing dumb to win his money, he and Fairfax duping a terrified Brewster.

The final moments of **Point Blank** are in the deserted ghost-prison Alcatraz, and teem with irony and ambiguity. Walker is back where he started, wised up, with a new friend and girl, to get the original $93,000. Again, the Alcatraz-run copter touches down, but the distrusting loner drops back this time, even as Brewster falls. Another ambush, perhaps with Walker's complicity, perhaps not. But the glib "businessman-criminal" who assumed Yost/Fairfax's execution is dead by the humorless conspirator. Now Yost/Fairfax does the offering, but Walker only withdraws further, perhaps correctly, as the rifleman emerges. This time around, Walker refuses to be drawn in. Now Yost/Fairfax appears to depart, leaving only the corpse and the money in the light, and no sign of Walker.

Besides seeing Walker's withdrawal as Orpheus' shadowy exit, vengeance complete, his retreat can be seen as yet a second defeat on the island, or at least a refusal to become further involved in a world of unlimited treachery and deception, and so of seemingly inevitable destruction. Walker, the canny individualist, has single-handedly outwitted the self-deluded "businessmen-criminals," but is is no match for a professional like Yost/Fairfax who is both a sly, bold schemer and an "honest" organization man. Beyond this, there are a number of wider social meanings that have been drawn from the film.

**Point Blank** is in fact more successful as social comment than real art. Though the Resnais subjective manipulation techniques are used with great power and beauty, the final effects are somewhat compromised by elements of TV style. As T.J. Ross (2.6) notes: "In each batch of shots there is a clear lesson, the practical message in all the mayhem, the gist of which is: watch out and never embark on anything on trust, particularly on anything to do with money." This tendency to telegraphy must be admitted, though the total message is clearly more complex.

John Boorman himself saw the film as dealing fundamentally with the plight of the individual in a mass society: "Walker was like an ordinary individual with no backing trying to deal with a business corporation or trying to claim from an insurance company and just being rejected and pushed away. And so he resorts to violence, which is the only thing to do in the face of blandness, I think – to punch somebody in the nose." (2.2) The director believes that in many ways "the business world *is* the Organization in America."

Alongside the plight of the individual, Boorman has taken a second theme, the denial of violence in society, the people on top refusing to deal with the frustrated anger of others. For the director, locking yourself in and refusing to recognize the violence on the streets seemed perhaps the heart of America, symbolized by the electrified fences guarding the beautiful homes he saw in Beverly Hills. The conservative Organization "chairmen" both react to Walker as if his bold rage was simply not allowed (Brewster: "Why do you go around doing things like that?").

Several critics noted these two themes and expanded on them. Brown (2.1) thinks the real center of **Point Blank** is in the theme of the individual versus society, and its consequences: "An increasingly common American lifestyle that unifies Dallas, Detroit, and Berkeley . . . the pressures in modern America that make violence and revolution "the only pure acts," the only way that a rebellion can be defined when the system reacts by absorbing and therefore nullifying all other protest . . . [yet it's shown] such individual revolution will never succeed, that the individual, in the last analysis, is powerless." Along the same chilling lines, Martin believed almost to the end that Yost/Fairfax was really a government agent, setting up the deaths because his department couldn't win a courtroom battle, the Feds pre-empting even the last resort (revolt).

Perhaps the most terrifying interpretation of the film is given by T.J. Ross (2.5). Ross sees the Lee Marvin character as simply an overt expression of the suburban subconscious: "Clearly, he knows his way around the City, through which he tours, however, with the detachment of a commuter. Yet it's not where he lives or finds his fate, but where he goes for his share of the plunder . . . For Walker is so familiar a specimen as to be nearly comfortable, his furious control recognizably that of the psychotic expert." Ross thinks Walker is simply an extreme case of middle class man at work, his motives totally monetary, his consciousness totally uninvolved, his emotional life totally autistic, his goal total self-sufficiency. Walker is simply "The Man in the Gray Flannel Suit, updated."

The versimilitude of *both* the Brown and Ross interpretations, opposed as they are, is fascinating. It suggests that very mythic power of Boorman's American creation. Walker is more than an archetypical rebel or bourgeois, he is an embodiment of the bitter, distrustful remorseless drive towards the truth which is survival, ready to pit himself for or against any "system" for what he must have, whose every move reveals the shabbiness, deceit and hypocrisy which American "Community" too often comes to.

# Jacques Demy

# THE MODEL SHOP

At the outset, Columbia Pictures' offer of a chance to make an American film seemed a panacea for the woes of Jacques Demy. Paris had somehow become dead for Demy, and the director began to feel he was "turning in circles" marking time. By contrast, his American experiences seemed interesting and important — all the 1968 turmoil over Black Power, Vietnam, youth — "I was completely fascinated, captivated by this kind of ferment. And the fact that I'd changed worlds, changed languages, opened my mind and gave me a new enthusiasm that I'd partly lost before." (3.2) In France, Demy had grown tired of his milieu. In America, he wanted to make a fresh start, to discover something.

Columbia Pictures' executive Jerry Ayers offered just that chance. Ayers had called to see Demy the day after he received the Academy Award for **The Umbrellas of Cherbourg** in 1966 to discuss the film and what had led to its production. The men subsequently corresponded, and during Demy's 1968 visit he told Ayers he was very much tempted to make a film in Los Angeles. Ayers told him: "Wonderful! Let's make a deal with Columbia!" and in a week it was settled, based on Demy's 10-page outline. Demy was given full responsibility for the film as scenarist and director-producer, working directly with the studio and thus having the maximum degree of freedom. **The Model Shop** would be a "below the line," small budget ($500,000) project, not including actors' salaries. Demy was even given "final cut" control, the power to set the exact final form of his film material. This is an unusual liberty for a studio supported filmmaker and Demy believes it was the result of the success of **Umbrellas of Cherbourg**, and the modesty (total costs plus publicity, about a million) of his project.

Demy wrote the script and practically all dialogue, then translated it — with help. "I tried to keep the same style as in France — very simple, efficient, and precise, to be clear and understood by everyone." (3.7) He rejected slang, which he thought would sound passe and dated only five years later. Straightforwardness was the

**45**

key: "The story of a man alone, a girl lost in town, I don't know — for writing that with your camera you only need the camera and an operator. And an actor, of course. Which means that with three people you could do that movie." (3.7)

But not in the United States. Shooting in Hollywood, Demy found himself saddled with several distinctly "American" problems. Union regulations required he work with a full crew, all skilled and professional, but often completely idle. Demy would leave his technicians out in the street somewhere, and hustle blocks away with his camera operator and Gary Lockwood to get shots of his man alone. The professionals were all highly efficient but, as with Antonioni, couldn't get used to the European's improvising — they had to be told days in advance or they were lost. Demy would have to ask for a certain specific travelling shot (moving camera shot) a week early. If he told them at the last minute, it might take half a day to shoot. The inertia was terrific.

Another difficulty was the studio's tendency to retain obsolete equipment, simply because it had been paid for and was serviceable. Demy and his cameraman Michael Hugo were forced to use an old Mitchell without a reflex viewfinder: "Very important because when you have to do a movement, and you want a very precise frame, you cannot get it right . . . it's awful to work like that instead of going through the lens and seeing exactly." (3.7) They found themselves introducing overhead quartz lights, a ten-year-old New Wave system for natural filming, to people who knew only how to work on sets. Though some equipment was superior to anything in Europe, the Hollywood moviolas and cutting tables were leftovers from the Chaplin days.

Finally, Demy was troubled by his French leading lady, Anouk Aimee, the star of **Lola** (1960) to which **The Model Shop** is a successor. "I wrote **Model Shop** with Anouk in mind — the same character as Lola, but seven years later. She came here with such a big head — and didn't show up the first day, never knew her lines; in France we would have fired her. But I will never work again with Aimee: Lola is dead now!" (3.7)

Nevertheless, Demy completed his 28-day shooting schedule losing only two days (one to Anouk, one to weather), and feels he has on the screen the story he wanted to tell, "a sort of loveless love story."

A melancholy piano theme. A squat gray oil pump on a beach in Venice, California: dark sand, shallow blue breakers, seagulls squawking, a grayhazed sky. The camera trucks down a blacktop road bordering the sea, showing wood and shingle beach houses, telephone poles, sandlots, more pumps enclosed in gray mesh boxes,

all in soft pastels. Finally, it turns at one clapboard beachhouse beside a throbbing pump, a green MG parked outside.

A rugged young man's face, red from sun and wind, muttering
in bed. Beside him a babyfaced, twentyish blonde pouts, smiles. She
turns to him, her voice high, with a suppressed edge: "You were
dreaming."

Barely awake: "Uh-huh?"

"Yes. You were talking in your sleep. You said love . . . nothing
else. Who were you dreaming of?"

"I don't know." His own voice is flat, dubious, questioning.

The bedroom is small, decorated mostly in psychedelia: a blue-
green poster, paper flowers, prints, a blue wig on an orange plastic
head and a teddy bear on the dressing table, a bra tossed on a chair.

In dark slacks, he strides to the door. A pinch-faced man iden-
tifies the young man as George Matthews (Gary Lockwood), and asks
for $100, or he'll repossess the MG. "If you'd shown some sign of
willingness . . . "

"He's just stallin' — why doncha just take the keys," grunts the
driver of the parked towtruck.

"What's the matter, he said he'd bring it in," Gloria (Alexandria
Hay) adds at the door. Her voice harsh, a thin chemise barely to her
thighs — "What a pair of Draculas!"

They'll give George till five. Inside, he lights a cigarette: "I got to
find a hundred bucks today."

Gloria shrugs: "Don't look at me. I already paid the gas and
phone bill." She makes breakfast in a silk robe and pink bikini while
George sorts possibilities: he already owes Robb fifty, he doesn't
want to call his mother.

Gloria: "You don't buy a $1500 car just because you like it.
You don't have a cent, you don't even work." Enthusiastic: "You
can go back to Hastings' — tell 'em you just got tired or something — "

"Yeah, but I don't wanna go, spend the rest of my life pushing
pencils for some architect." George looks happy: "You know what
I want — "

"Yes, I know what you want, you want to rebuild the Empire
State Building, only higher and in polished aluminum." She's heard
it all before.

"Try red copper," George mutters. They sit on the screened-in
porch, the pistoning pump against the hazy sea.

Gloria, reasonably: "Okay, so you've got ideas. You don't become an architect overnight. Nobody is gonna give a million to a
guy of twenty-six just because he's got ideas."

"Crap . . . I should kill my time at Hastings' till the draft."

Gloria gives up. In the bedroom she combs out her peroxided

hair and straps on heels: "Jerry's picking me up. They're looking for girls for TV commercials. At least he shows some interest in my career *which* I appreciate *and* is a little more than you do."

She slips on a very short black dress and inspects herself past the big teddy bear on the dresser, then turns to George, soft-voiced, her eyes concerned: "I've been living with you for over a year, George. I said I'd live with you for six months, remember? So we could be sure if we still loved each other . . . after that, I asked you if you would marry me and you said *no* — that marriage was only an empty convention and not worth the paper it was printed on. I said okay, fine. Later I asked you for a child. I said I really needed a child, George, and you said you weren't prepared for the responsibility. Well, I have waited. At least I should know who you are, what you want, what you're living for. You reject society. You refuse to commit yourself to anything or anybody, not even to me. Am I wrong?"

"No, you're not wrong."

She picks up her beaded bag while George pulls on a dark t-shirt and jams his wallet in his pocket. "I hate this kind of conversation," he mutters, and goes out to the bright bottle-green roadster under the open sky. Gloria leans on the windscreen: "George . . . what would you say if we went our separate ways from now on? . . . Well, what d'ya think?"

George doesn't answer, but guns the little MG out onto the blacktop road, red radiator and wire wheels glinting . . .

He cruises through Los Angeles. By starting at the sea and muting the colors to pastel, Demy turns the inferno of Antonioni and Boorman into a gentle seacoast town. There is no sound but the melancholy piano theme: a chord, three slow wandering single notes, then three warmer, closer chords, varied and embellished. George drives silently past boulevards full of drug stores, banks, gas stations, pulling in at a parking lot. A big nosed, cheerful young man named Robb greets him, but asks for his original fifty first: "Color TV — Jane just had to have it, y'know what I mean."

A calm, lovely woman in white dress, shoes, scarf, asks breathlessly for her car in a French accent. In dark glasses she studies George as he lights her cigarette, leaves in a big creamy Mercury convertible. "Interested? Your friend Gloria wouldn't like it . . . " George zips out.

His strong young face in closeups, George follows, catching up in traffic, climbing up through sudden hills to the Rimsky-Korsakov "Scheherazade Theme." It is still early, the day is bright under blue skies. The woman stops for a moment to study him calmly in her rearview mirror, then continues up along scrub-covered slopes to park and disappear inside a big, vaguely Georgian house. The

Scheherazade Theme is suddenly cut off, but as George edges round the house to study the immense city spreading to the horizon in the basin, the rich romantic music surges up again . . .

Zipping back, George picks up a teenage girl in serape, pants and boots: "You can drop me on the strip." The car radio bangs: "Washington!-Paris-has-been-selected-as-site-of-Vietnamese-peace-talks!" The girl rolls a marijuana joint as they drive into the basin, offering it as she gets out. George turns on acid rock . . .

Inside a quiet old stucco house, an acid rock group called Spirit greet George at rehearsal's end: guitars, drums, amplifiers, love beads, flowered shirts, shoulder hair, organ grinder mustache, shaved head, and a gentle blonde girl holding a naked baby in the big plain living room. George's happy friend seats him in a massive old armchair while the others shamble out, plays a variation on the film's own theme: "Haven't got the words down yet . . . a sort of testimony to the insanity of this world." George slumps, eyes slitted, not really interested, even when he gets the $100 without hesitation. He murmurs of his own creative urge, of the 20-year wait for seniority, going around in circles like — "I did an incredible thing. I was in my car and I started to follow this — " he hesitates. "Now, nothing! . . . I stopped at this place that overlooks the whole city. I suddenly felt *exhilarated* — I was really moved by the geometry of the place, its conceptions, its Baroque harmony. It's really pure poetry! I want to build something like that, create something . . . " Making excuses, George rushes away . . .

Up to park before the big white house, touching the great round brass handles on the doors. He buttons the intercom: "I want to talk to the lady — " A crone's voice: "Nobody home, nobody came!" For a moment the woman peers from an upstairs window, then the house stands opaque, closed. The dark figure does not look at the vista again, but U-turns and races downhill . . .

To a shabby grid of downtown streets: gas stations, abandoned stores, loft buildings, trashbins, a storefront poolroom with jukebox, drab idlers, Hell's Angels. At the counter, George peruses an underground paper: articles like "Law Against Marijuana Unfair," personals starting "If You Hate Sex . . . " and "For French Studies, call —." He turns as the lovely woman in white, still hidden by dark glasses, passes. George scurries down the block to see her enter a storefront "Model Studio," the glass painted red but for a woman's curvaceous white silhouette, and notices: Rent A Girl, Free Film. George follows, through a red door . . .

Inside, a young blonde in boots, miniskirt, and a frilly low-cut blouse looks up brightly from a portable TV. "Hello! Do you want to take some pictures?" The walls are draped in red and purple, suggestively taped with a few *Playboy* pinups. She shows an album

Lola (Anouk Aimee) poses in the model shop.

with eight by ten signed glossies of the girls in provocative poses. "You know our terms — $20 for half an hour, $12 for fifteen minutes." The TV mutters. George finds the woman in white; net stockinged, legs drawn up and a shy smile. "I like this one." He gives her a fifty, gets a camera and change. "Push here, turn there."

The young man follows her down dark zigzag corridors, one wall raw brick, the other partitioned into rooms with beaded curtains. Electronic guitars whisper. "She'll be in in a minute."

George drifts around the room: green and silvery tulipped wallpaper, a big bed with a furry coverlet, a wooden rocker, lightstands.

The bead curtain sways aside as Lola (Anouk Aimee) steps into the room, her cool, ethereal beauty finally revealed. She smiles, her voice husky, exotic, breathless: "Hi!" With a touch of mockery, she moves gracefully to a wooden stand hung with props: "What would you like? Boots? Hat? Or whip? Take your choice." She is always charmingly breathless.

Now, in silence, the beautiful woman poses, shifts, poses again around the sensuous room. First seated sideways in the rocker, one arm high, to cradle her head, face provocatively pouting. Now a lovely expression of repose, her neck rising from the boa's feathery foam. In the camera viewfinder: golden brown skin, dark flashing eyes, good mouth, the cloud of the boa shifting and twirling, her face between shots coolly lovely. George is mute, framing her in soft clouds of pink, white, blue, Lola shifting the lightstand herself. "Would you like me on the bed now?" She sits with curled-up knees, grins provocatively over one fine shoulder, lies delicately across the coverlet, always self-possessed: "You are not very demanding, nor very talkative either . . . but it's all right with me . . . you have just one left. Do you want me to do anything?"

"I like what I've got," George says, zipping her back into the white dress. I'm more interested in you." Flatly: "It's kind of degrading work, isn't it? Why do you do it?"

Lola regards him clearly: "To make my living. But I don't like this word degrading," she says without scorn. "After all, I don't know what you do to make your living."

George does nothing at the moment.

"Then you don't run the risk of degrading yourself by working," she comments with a smile. She stands at the curtain, studying him.

"I followed you this morning."

"Yes, I know . . . goodbye."

George drives to a photoshop, jammed with gadgets, run by a man in frilly shirt and tuxedo. He wants to know if the girl was pretty. "I just prefer it."

In closeups George's bluntfeatured young face, red from sun and wind, now blue bearded, stares ahead as he tools through the city.

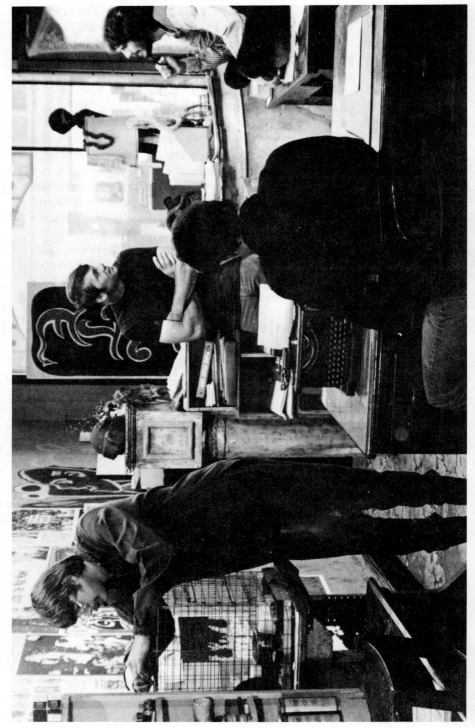

George (Gary Lockwood) visits the underground newspaper called "The Paisley."

On the radio, acid rock shambles to electronic guitars:
> *I had nothin' to lose,*
> *and little to say.*
> *I couldn't understand your leavin'*
> *or believe you'd be gone,*
> *the very next day.*

At the Blackstone Finance Company for the first time we see men in business suits, desks and typewriters, a disconcerting purposefulness. George argues without conviction with a middle-aged executive secretary, then slips out, trailing excuses. "He's going to get the money," the lady explains. "It'll be a surprise," an agent comments drily. "We'll get the car in the morning." . . .

On the boulevard, George is stopped at a light with an ancient Chevy painted in psychedelic yellows and blues and mild flame shapes. A young voice: "Hey, George, we're going to The Paisley — " . . .

The Paisley is an underground paper housed in another storefront. Around a cluster of desks topped with paperwork and a very old typewriter are more casual not-quite-young people: one on a table in full lotus, another with long hair, fatigues, and his arm in a cast, an editor type: "It's beautiful, getting better all the time — circulation hit 90,000 but money's still the real problem."

George: "You guys make me feel right at home."

"Hey, come work here on the paper . . . it'll give you enough bread to get by on. If you like it, you stay — if you don't, you're free." On the bright yellow walls are tacked proofs with blank columns and space, old cabinets, a typesetting frame with a silent black working at it. (One critic comments that the soft hazy light makes the hippy youths look like bearded angels.)

They exchange draft statuses, wonder about peace talks: "The Korean talks took two years — these guys may take six months just to sharpen their pencils — "

George calls his parents, leaning against a Belmondo poster. His run-ragged-mother: "I already sent as much as I can." "Yeah, I know, but couldn't you send two hundred dollars."

George's father, bluffly hearty: "Here's the word, George . . . " In closeup there is only George and the phone. "You're to report up here this coming Monday . . . make the best job you can . . . right attitude . . . damn good time out of it . . . I had some good times in the Pacific."

George, almost tearfully: "Yeah, I know. I could die."

Mildly reproving: "You sound like a coward, George."

George backs away: "This whole conversation is ridiculous. I just don't think we're gonna be able to understand each other at all." He hangs up, and turns to the journalists with his news. Upset but

George (Gary Lockwood) argues when Gloria (Alexandria Hay) confronts him with the photographs.

vague: "I'm scared. Like it's really a death sentence. It's the first time I've ever really thought about it. Death, you know. It's insane."

"Yeah, well . . . " "If there's anything I can do . . . " George goes out . . .

To a Brahms' duet for strings and harpsichords, George calls for his photos. In the early evening, under the neons, he studies them, mostly blurry and badly composed, but at least one with Lola's beauteous, clear face regarding him. He hides her from the gas attendant as he did from his musician friend, then through the deepening night speeds back to the beachhouse, opening beer and sprawling in the cluttered bedroom to stare at the gentle romantic woman, dragging on the teenager's gift. The room is gloomy away from the harsh night light. In flashing contrast, we see the amber brown Lola in the camera's soft focus, wrapped or drifting against clouds of Schubert pink, magenta, steel blue. Outside, a sportscar engine revs down. Door noises, and George jams the pictures in the dressing table.

Gloria comes in in raincoat and packages. Politely: "Home long, George?" Excitedly: "I think I got it! The part! They're gonna test me tomorrow, isn't it fabulous . . . well, you don't seem very pleased . . . " She hangs on his neck, ecstatic: "Jerry was really beautiful and so was his uncle — he's this real distinguished type, fifty, gray hair, crew cut, three phones — know what I mean!" She fusses with the morning dishes, a bowl of peaches for now.

"His uncle saw my picture and called the director immediately. It was *incredible*! He was really excited."

George, his voice husky: "What's his proposition?"

A shade defensive: "What d'ya mean, proposition? . . . It isn't really a *part* . . . it's a series of commercials for a revolutionary soap — it makes bubbles, not foam, bubbles!"

Framed in the doorway, George studies the tight excited little blonde. Skeptically: "Well, bubbles or not, he'd make it in a bathtub and I can see it now."

"I can name a lot of actresses who started that way. Thank God I'm still pretty enough to be seen naked in a bathtub. Maybe somebody important'll notice me — and what about *you*, what did you accomplish today? Did you pay off those creeps?" She strides into the bedroom to change.

Thumbs in pockets, George calls: "No I didn't see Robb, nothing. In fact he asked me to pay him back. David needs somebody at the newspaper, but it's too late, I haven't told you what else happened — "

Furious, legs scissoring, tightfaced, Gloria comes out: *"Yes, I can see! Whose little trick is this?"* She clutches the photos.

George struggles with her as she rips.

"What're you playing around with, whores now, George? . . . *Let go of me! . . .* It's disgusting! . . . *And I trusted you!*" They bump and struggle together, "Get away from me George. I don't want to see you again, ever."

With sudden dignity: "Don't worry about it. I'll be leaving tomorrow. I received my draft notice. I have to be in San Francisco Monday morning."

Gloria, contrite: "I'm sorry."

"Why? You wanted us to break up." On his knees he searches for pieces.

"Yeah, but — I, oh, never mind." Hands on hips, she regards him distrustfully.

Jerry comes in, a junior-grade amiable Tab Hunter with sculpted blonde poll, deep-tan, sports jacket, ascot: "Hi! The film starts at 7:00 — "

"Uh, George won't be coming with us."

Sympathetic: "If you want to stay with George, we could make it tomorrow night." But she's ready, and off they zoom . . .

To the wandering piano theme, George drives through the night city, neon signs glowing softly like the light through the beaded curtains. The blonde puts new film in his camera ("I love the smell, don't you?") and they move through the corridors, George's expression strained. "You know . . . you're cute," the blonde twinkles.

It's a different room, with a couch, a big plaster cupid holding a vase, tinny chandelier with colored bulbs, papered in pale green and yellow. The beads move aside, and again that loveliness, that cool husky richness: "Why did you come back?"

"I wanted to see you."

Lola brushes past, still in white, reaching for the zipper, concerned: "Your pictures must have been awful, you looked so awkward . . . I hope this time will be better."

"I didn't come here to take pictures . . . " They regard each other for a moment . . .

"Why did you follow me?" she rushes.

"Because I wanted to know who you were. Why didn't you look at me?"

"You're kidding," she husks. "You know very well that most men who follow girls in the street are . . . sadists . . . maniacs . . . nuts."

George cuts back: "The first time I saw you comin' in this, uh, tart factory, I was surprised. I wondered what kind of woman you were . . . then I thought, what the hell!"

For the first time, her voice is cold: "If you came here to insult me, you can leave right now." Then, helplessly: "Whether I get undressed in this room in front of you, or on the beach, what's the

**56**

difference? Men look at me the same way . . . and it's the only job I could get without a work permit. In four days I'll have what I need for my airline ticket." She shudders. "I was completely broke."

"It's too bad you're leaving," George tells her flatly. "I would really have liked to see you again. I'm leaving tomorrow, I'm going into the army." For a moment the two seem half-siblings, lean, tanned shapes with bared arms, one in blue, one white. "Let's not leave on that note. Let's have a drink."

She regards herself in the mirror, touches her hair. "Ah, you're sweet . . . "

"Are you anxious to get back to France?"

"Yes," she answers ingenuously, "but at the same time it . . . makes me sad. I made good friends here. And I love the city."

"Most people hate it. But now there're two of us who like it — that's good enough reason to have a drink."

She smiles: "If it will make you happy — "

"Hey, you forgot your pictures!" the blonde calls to a rushing George.

In the parking lot, George's roadster points right in the foreground, Lola's big creamy convertible the other way behind it. Lola is wearing her white scarf but we see her eyes: "I feel a little stupid," she murmurs. "Not really, but I'm here, waiting to follow you, and I don't even know your name."

"Very well," George replies. "My name is George Matthews and I was born in — " George ticks off studying architecture, his draft notice, his parents.

Lola smiles: "My real name is Cissy. Lola is a stage name. I was born a few years before you — really very few." She sighs shyly. "I lived in Nantes a long time, then in Paris. I moved around a lot. I have a son who is grown who is waiting for me in Paris. I miss him very much."

"Is he the reason you're going back?"

"Yes . . . he's all that's really waiting for me."

George holds the wheel with both hands: "Cecile, I want to say something. I know it'll sound totally crazy and I never said it before because I . . . really never felt it before. But I love you."

Lola smiles nervously, and tells him: "You're very nice . . . and what you say is very moving . . . but you don't know me at all. You saw me in the street — you followed me — you took pictures of me — you insulted me — and now you love me . . . it can't be very serious, can it?"

"Maybe I need you."

"Me also. Or else you needed to talk."

"And I needed to say 'I love you.' That's true." George's voice goes brusque: "But I guess that's a sentiment you don't have room for in the kind of life that you live."

Stung: "Here you are insulting me again."

"No . . . *forget it*. I was mistaken. Excuse me — goodbye!"

On the loom of neoned streets, Lola's big white convertible pauses for a light. As that morning, George pulls up halfway behind her: "There's been a misunderstanding."

Lola doesn't hesitate: "Will you come to my place? We can have a drink there." The little roadster follows the big white car . . .

On a modest shaded street, George follows the radiant woman towards a bungalow. "I live here with Barbara, a friend of mine, and have to return her car. I'm always afraid to be late. She works on Sunset at night. Thanks to her I've been able to stay. She found me the job at the Model Shop."

Barbara meets her at the door, a shapely black in a yellow dress and Afro with a little high voice; the two girls are pleased to see each other. Halfway through the door, Barbara calls: "There's some Scotch behind the bar. Have a good time! Bye!"

"She's lovely, isn't she!" Lola exclaims. Nervously: "She helped me so much when she met me — that was last summer in New York after my divorce — I couldn't stop crying — for six months I cried — I couldn't speak to anyone — a friend — a waiter in a restaurant — without starting to cry — "

She turns on a record, goes for the Scotch. The living room is painfully garish: a black-studded sofa, a plastic bar with two stools, a cheap hi-fi, inflated vinyl pillows, posters about pot.

"Did you love him very much?"

"If the word love has any meaning at all, it's not strong enough to express what I felt for him — you see I had waited — a long time for Michael — I gave him everything — I always trusted him — then, three years ago, we came to America — do I bore you?"

"No, please go on."

She smiles warmly, then apologizing, gets the ice. "He met a girl named Jackie — a Frenchwoman who was living in Las Vegas and spent every hour gambling — I thought he was taking business trips — actually he was gambling with this woman — but he was not in love with her — Michael — gambled for the money — he loved money — perhaps more than anything." She pauses a moment, then quickly, getting it over with: "Later, he lost everything — we didn't have a cent — so I started to work again — we fought constantly — we decided to call it quits — oh, without any question it was a greater disappointment of mine . . . "

George, in his flat, well-meaning tones: "But you could meet someone else . . . build some kind of life for yourself . . . "

Lola brings her shoulders back, stares at him ingenuously: "But you don't believe me — Michael took everything — I am empty — I

George (Gary Lockwood) agonizingly argues with Lola (Anouk Aimee).

don't want to love anyone — ever again — you understand?"

George struggles with her idea: "You're going to become a . . . sad old gal."

Lola gives a weak, Continental shrug, smiles: "Ah? — I didn't mean I won't have affairs — that's different!"

She stands over the film's second photo album with George. Beneath the glossy plastic is a stocky blonde man with a boy who shares his features. "Michael . . . and my son when he was seven."

The next picture is the vibrant young Lola of the Model Shop still, net stockinged legs drawn up and gay smile: "That's me in Nantes — I used to sing — not very well — but, you know . . . "

A rugged plain-featured man in sailor whites, the boy atop one shoulder: "That's Frankie — an American friend — he was killed in Vietnam at the beginning of the war — it's horrible, isn't it. I'd met him in France . . . "

"Do you think you'll ever come back here again?"

Lola, bemused by the recollections: "Oh, perhaps — I don't know — I don't like to look ahead, to make plans — don't you ever feel like that?"

George is at home again: "Mmm, I'm luckier than that. My life's been beautifully organized for me — a well planned trip . . . You know I realized today I'm afraid of death . . . what's more beautiful than life — maybe the reflections of life — a book, concert, sculpture . . . I wanted to build, construct . . . but man's only thriving passion is to destroy . . . is it worth the struggle?"

Lola, vigorous, huskily: "But that is cowardly — I've survived life, struggling, hoping — and love has tried to destroy those hopes — but it doesn't matter, I never gave up."

"Yeah, but you won't let yourself love anymore," George argues out doggedly. "That's giving up."

"But I was shattered!" the beautiful woman exclaims.

George shrugs.

Lola, quickly, drawn in yet wise: "Now I'm the one who is wrong — and I know I'm wrong."

George intensely, letting himself go: "If I said — even though we can't believe in love anymore, you and I — if I said let's try to create something for each other — I need you, you can help me — would you refuse?"

Lola, to a child: "But I don't love you."

George, not pausing for either's reasonableness: "Would you refuse to help me?"

Lola, slowly: "No . . . I wouldn't refuse . . . " But she crosses her arms in front of her.

"I need help, I'm asking you to help me." His voice is hurt.

"You're a child."

Carried along willy-nilly, his voice upset, but never doubting: "All right then, I need your help like a child, I need to be loved like a child."

Lola nervously moves towards the door. Huskily: "Please leave now."

George, half hurt, half adolescently challenging: "I don't want to leave, I want to stay with you, I want to spend the night with you — you don't love me, you don't have to love me." Clumsily, mocking: "Let's just chalk it up as one more affair for you, you've had affairs since your divorce, haven't you?"

Lola, turning away: "Please don't talk to me about that — go away!"

"Answer me! You've had affairs since your divorce — yes or no!"

Huskily deep: " . . . yes."

George is at the door, Lola's back to us. Plunging on: "Then why not me! I told you I only want to love you! . . . Because you're afraid!"

Lola, husky, angry, excited, agonized: "Yes, I'm afraid. I'm afraid of one more affair, one more love. I don't want either you nor anyone else anymore." Suddenly she moves towards him: "George!" . . .

A masculine hand's fingertip traces a curve from a slim ankle up along an elegant calf to a lovely knee. George: "Serenity . . . fairness . . . it's like perfection . . . I can't explain it, it's like your shoulder curves, the straight line of your neck — pure joy . . . you make me believe everything is possible."

A low camera captures them staring softly at each other in bed, heads propped on bent arms. Lola husks: "You really speak as if you were just discovering love. As if you never loved anyone . . . "

Now they are shown alone for each line.

"I never loved anyone."

"I don't believe you."

"Why?"

She holds up his gnawed fingertips: "Because you bite your nails."

George offers the money towards airfare to Paris and they are further apart, Lola grooming herself while George lies there: "If I accept this money, you'll lose me — "

"I'll lose you anyway," George says flatly. Lola moves out of the frame. George offers his cigarettes — they're back at the beginning.

Lola, dressed, brushes her hair, staring into the mirror at the rich chestnut cascade. Shyly: "You know, last night — I said yes, but it was not true — I lived alone." Again he zips up the white dress.

"Why me?"

Lola smiles: "Why? Why? Do you always find a reason for everything you do? . . . you're lucky."

George would have her stay in Los Angeles. "If you stay . . . I'll stay too. I'll desert for love. Love's a good cause . . . "

But neither continues, the subject is dropped. In his t-shirt and jeans George follows her to the living room. Faintly the sounds of children, laughing, gay shrillness filtering in. George gives her his money.

"I feel like you're paying me for the night . . . why are you doing this?"

George laughs: does she always find answers to all her questions? She'll call . . . and see him tonight . . .

George zips through the paisley morning's delicate sunlight, along the blacktop seaside road. Even the radio bangs good news: "the-bombings-may-be-halted-and-even-a-ceasefire-may-be-called-"
George rushes happily home.

In the ramshackled beachhouse, Gloria stands in a short pink dress with a red flight suitcase, the teddy under her arm. "I waited all night. You could have *called* me. I realized you probably found something *better*." In a sexy voice: "You were with that chick, weren't you?"

Bothered, George tells her to shut up.

"No, I want you to know just how much — oh you've really hurt me, George!" The little baby-faced blonde, her eyes dark-ringed, but dry, looks at him reproachfully: "Never mind. It's just — getting used to the idea of not seeing you anymore. Maybe it's good — I don't think I'd ever have had the courage to leave — it'll work out. I'll end up by forgetting."

"I never meant to hurt you." George's thumbs are back in his pockets.

A jet roars over, Jerry calls: "He's coming to pick me up, I'm moving into his place . . . what do you care if I love him " She zips the plastic suitcase, checks her face in the mirror.

"Don't act tough."

Gloria's voice goes soft, she looks at him as she did a morning before: "I'm not being tough, I'm just disappointed. I thought you'd make an effort so things would work out. A simple happy life. I didn't know that you didn't want it, that you didn't love me anymore . . . I'm a little bit stupid, huh?"

She won't live there without him: "Goodbye, George."

"Goodbye, Gloria." The Porsche rushes away, as another jet vacuum-cleaners over.

George walks through the house, looks at the empty bed, suddenly reaches for the wallphone. A highpitched voice answers: "Oh, Barbara, this is George . . . I wanted to speak with Lola." But she borrowed money from Barbara and has already left. George's voice is flat and doubtful as always, but has a pained note now which could not be recognized before. "I didn't have anything special to say . . . I just wanted to wish her good luck . . . " Outside, the tow trucker is hitching up the roadster, hauls it off. George doesn't look. "That's good, yeah, she made me very happy . . . No, I just wanted to tell her that I loved her . . . " Demy closes in to the blued, tanned face with its young strong features, eyes shuttered. "I just wanted to let her know that I was going to try and begin again, you know what I mean? That I, I just wanted her to know that I was gonna try — " A jet drowns his voice. "Yah, sounds stupid, doesn't it, but I can't — " The picture is slowly dissolving to a blue frame, the voice goes on: "You know, a person can't always try, y'know, yeah, always try, yeah, always try . . . " The last sound is the film's piano theme: a chord, three wandering notes, three simpler chords together . . .

Since his first film, **Lola**, Jacques Demy has tried to link his creations, with a few ongoing characters. **Lola** for Pauline Kael was "like an adolescent's dream of romance, formed from old movies . . . Lola, abandoned by her sailor lover, brings up their child in the best sentimental tradition . . . and he does return, fabulously rich and still in love with her, and they drive off into a bright future." (3.4) Michael, Lola, and Frankie all appear in the first film. Jackie is Jeanne Moreau in Demy's **Bay of Angels**, and now all four have been linked.

Demy's approach to **The Model Shop** is very different from the earlier films however, which all have a consistent romantic and sentimental style. The filmmaker has stated he wanted "to forget myself and be the sort of guy who's just here with a fresh eye and tries to speak of something that is new to him, and appears to him to be fantastically interesting." (3.2) He thinks he could have called the film **Los Angeles, '68**.

George's odyssey in search of a hundred dollars is a collage of the new life styles and how they work: careerless, cashless living (George and Gloria); low status, low pressure jobs (Robb's car lot); teenage autonomy (the hitchhiker); communal living (the Spirit); merchandizing sexuality (The Model Shop); interracial living (Barbara and Lola). Demy shows the new alternatives and compromises in action, without adulation or mockery, and along with them the "old fashioned" money and success oriented youngsters like Gloria and Jerry, likeable and kindly in their way. Kael complains (3.4) that Demy's view of American youth is amateurish, shallow and flaccid; he misses the humor of Gloria's asking for a baby so George will be committed to something, or "anything ironic in the rock musicians' casting themselves and sealing themselves in the life style of sweet Jesus." Though there is black humor here, the incidents are not basically amusing, and Demy chooses to dwell on their simple factuality.

Yet **The Model Shop** is clearly not a straightforward documentary. Much of it is lyrical and romantic — the remaking of Los Angeles into a gentle seaside town, George's awkward painful approaches to the Frenchwoman, Lola's unhappy ingenuousness. Still other parts seem wooden — George's dragging coffeehouse philosophy and undefined alienation, Gloria's restless demanding practicality, Lola's brittle emptiness. To be consistent, **The Model Shop** seems at heart a perceptive documentary of emotional textures of patterns of mood and feeling setting off or contrasting each other.

Central to all this is George, who Pauline Kael grudgingly admits is a new American type. Graduate schools, drop out pools like San Francisco and the welfare department, and "creative" workshops are maddeningly full of Georges — the nice, vague, bright, sexualized children of the middle class with degrees and affairs and other credentials, but who are nevertheless seemingly largely helpless, aimless, and ineffective at making life real for themselves. Far more than Antonioni's crazily rebellious Mark, or any campus bomb-builder, George represents the characteristic plight of many young Americans, atypical only for his drift into the draft, which most Georges slide around simply without reflection as an unpleasant waste of time. Facing a crisis, George is hardly aware of his own feelings except as abstracted death fears and vague humanistic yearnings. Real action is unthinkable, except on a childish impulsive level. He can't seem to care about anything.

George's peculiar fascination as a young middle-class product is in the distrustful, passionate, secretive child revealed inside the agreeable uncommunicative vague young man. Fairly early, it's clear that George can be perceptive, knowing, and socially skillful — he's slept with a pretty starlet for a year with no special efforts, lived happily on his own with many friends, is a qualified professional. But now he has to act, and won't; Gloria, friends, car just don't count, were part of some middle-class package deal he didn't really want. Canby calls the model shop "a house of prostitution for the inhibited." George's life has likewise been a model shop, where he never tried to really connect, but held back his secret self, a handsome, private dreamer. "A simple happy life," Gloria sums up, "I didn't know you didn't want it."

His meeting with Lola somehow touches George, and the rest of the film shows his painful half attempt to somehow "get himself together." He deals with Lola with a terrible desperate urgency, pressing for her acceptance if only as a child, trying to solve her own problems with clumsy "emotional logic." He faces up to Gloria, coming out with his dislike of her career, later expressing affection, but letting the affair end when he could have held her. The new George appears more vulnerable and defensive: he doesn't conceal the pictures, one-ups Gloria's anger with his draft notice, won't really desert, and can't keep the desperate, frightened Lola from fleeing.

Considered as the documentation of George's first weak steps towards completeness and self awareness, **The Model Shop** is very effective. George's stoical vagueness and coffeehouse meanderings have an almost pathological tension; he drives in circles diverted by the complex music of his private self.

The same tension between George's outward amiability and his barely concealed self-disgust is reflected throughout the film. Despite their friendliness and liberation, George will not speak of Lola to Robb, his rock musician friend, or Gloria. She is part of his private self. Demy suggests that the new life styles, ingenuous and open as they are, may not really accommodate the problems of the transition generation, nor perhaps ever deal with all the complexities of human nature. George's lack of response to his friends' concern about him, and especially about his coming induction, shows his stultified closeness, while in fact the "alternate culture" seems to have little energy or skill at dealing with even this mundane threat.

George's tension appears most dramatically in his dealings with Gloria and Lola. While Pauline Kael writes off **The Model Shop** as another "trying-to-appeal-to-youth-movie," its real progenitor is Hitchcock's **Vertigo**. Like Hitchcock's Midge, Gloria is subtly shaped by George into a realistic, assertive, career girl — she has to get ahead to pay her share, and inevitably nags and grows dissatisfied. George is dazzled by the affectionate Lola, whose exoticism resembles that of **Vertigo**'s Madeleine, and similarly subdues her. ("A sentiment you don't have room for . . . let's try to create something . . . Chalk it up as one more affair.") George half-consciously manipulates both relationships, discouraging any seeds of romanticism in Gloria, while asserting his ethereal attraction for Lola as a desperate need: "I can't explain it," he says after their night together, "You make everything possible."

George has spun the magic out into an answer. But his talk of desertion and a life together is faltering and inconclusive, and in the end he loses both girls, perhaps half-deliberately: Gloria has drifted off to someone who wants her, even as a careerist; and George gives Lola enough money so she can impulsively flee. The last shots of George on the phone suggest he's slipped back into the trap of amiable emptiness — perhaps with the loss of girls and car and freedom, perhaps only until he can assimilate the night of desperately needed love, perhaps with a terrible half-awareness of self-betrayal. But in any case, this is not the easy way out into-the-sunset-together or blame-putting of many youth movies.

The American role of Lola in **The Model Shop** is hard to interpret. She is admittedly ungainly as a lewd photographer's model, and Demy's insisting on her reciting her story is tedious. (Some critics find the line "Do I bore you?" Demy's own tipoff.) But Lola is clearly not just dragged in to give George the will to go on. He is the one to argue her around, and given half a chance, she panics into returning to France. Her love stories, lovely radiance of movement and expression, and calm and gentle openness do produce an ambiance, a sense of wonder and acceptance alien to flat-voice, pretty, dollar-hungry, casual Southern California. It is a mood of mysteries and fulfillments in the world ("Do you always find a reason? . . . You speak as if you were just discovering love . . . love's not strong enough to express what I felt."). It's notable that neither Lola's appearance (the drive to the white house) nor her vanishing (the sudden flight) are clearly explained. Interpreted as a symbol, she could be life, ephemeral, ethereal, wise, loving, mysterious, and full of possibilities. This time George lets her get away.

# Milos Forman

# TAKING OFF

**Taking Off**'s "real life" beginning is the most dramatic of any of the included films — the danger of Soviet arrest and trial to its director, Milos Forman. His modest but successful **Fireman's Ball** had been co-produced by the Czech government and Carlo Ponti. When Ponti withdrew his $80,000 investment, the State Bank blamed Forman for the currency loss. Under the Novotny regime, the situation looked grim. Forman screened **Fireman's Ball** for producer-director Claude-Berry in Paris, and fortunately new backers were recruited. In passing, Forman mentioned his idea for an American film.

The way Forman tells it (4.4) Berry happily arranged "the best agent of the best agency in the world" for him, and in March, 1968, the Czech director and his friend Jean-Claude Carriere began the script in New York. Its progress bizarrely prefigures the whole project's hegira; for it was just weeks before the turmoil of Martin Luther King's death made Forman shift to Paris, which was pleasant and quiet. Until May, Forman was stubborn, pushing on despite strikes, riots and incipient chaos until August, when he gave up and went back to Prague. More bad timing. But in October, 1968, the script was completed.

All along, Forman had been cheered by the interest of Paramount Pictures. But, except for Bob Evans ("It is so good! So funny! . . . But maybe I am wrong!"), the Paramount executives all disliked the script. Forman found their arguments eerie parallels to criticism of his work during the worst Stalinist period at home: "You want to make people laugh, but you don't laugh with them. You laugh against them, and they don't like it!" (Indeed, this is an elegant statement of the "formalist vs. socialist realist" conflict in Soviet film.) But though nobody much liked it, all the Paramount people told Forman they were eager to make his film.

Forman and Jean-Claude Carriere went ahead with a definitive script, John Klein checking their English. Paramount's decision: the script was so bad they weren't interested — but would Forman direct **Galileo** with Rod Steiger in Italy? Forman wanted to make his own script, and would make a deal with someone else.

The director suspects that Paramount's money crisis had made them shy of anything but a sure winner, though they were too cagey to admit it. He would contrast the mendacity and double dealing of the Hollywood moguls with the very open and ethical Czech film industry under the Novotny yoke. He credits this to the smaller financial stakes, and each individual's dependence on the good will of his fellows for survival.

After several more Alice-in-Wonderland incidents, Joseph Levine offered to handle the project, with Sidney Lumet as producer (Forman much admires Lumet's **Twelve Angry Men**). Levine agreed to a film with a budget below $1.2 million.

There was one problem. To forfeit the script, Paramount wanted $140,000 in pre-production costs (including $50,000 bonus Forman's agent had wangled, picture or no). But no matter how it was figured, Forman's film couldn't be made for under $1.3 million, Paramount's money included. After hard bargaining, Paramount agreed to half the money now. Lumet's and Forman's salaries were trimmed. Final budget: $1,225,000. But Levine wouldn't put in the odd $25,000 and Paramount wouldn't wait for it. Finally, Forman and Lumet cut the $25,000 from their wages. But now Levine was having second thoughts . . .

Forman kept going. "Keep trying, be stubborn" is his advice to aspiring filmmakers, and it worked. Ned Tanen's fledgling film program at Universal took on **Taking Off** for under a million (4.1). The program would pay Forman a percentage instead of a big salary; if the film did well, so would he.

But probably the real attraction was Tanen's hands-off policy: the finance company would put up the money, cross its fingers, and let the filmmaker have unrestricted freedom in production. Forman could appreciate that.

The director returned to New York City to write the final version of his script with John Gueras, spending a lot of time walking around, taping the conversation of young people in the Village.

He also began casting. Lyn Carlin was chosen after seeing her in **Faces.** Buck Henry was recruited to help with the (re)writing, but after a couple of hours Forman decided he was just right for the tragic-comic father role. Other parts were filled by non-professionals, people chosen after long hours spent studying faces in Greenwich Village, the East Village, Central Park — Lynnea Heacock, the fifteen-year-old girl runaway heroine, was discovered in a water fight at the Bethesda Fountain. Forman's search for the proper ambiance of expressions and behavior led to filming at a joyless Grossinger's singles weekend — one with nobody under forty. The funereal faces were the backdrop for the desperate gaiety of the runaway's parents.

Forman's way of directing is to wait and only break down the scenes on the set, deciding the numbers of shots and takes after getting set up with his real actors. As with Antonioni, this approach sometimes led to problems, for the crew always wanted the next day's first set up. "But it didn't make things difficult for me," Forman commented, "because I just didn't tell them."

Forman's approach also forbids the actors to ever see the script. He simply tells them where to sit and what to say in each shot. Sometimes the improvisation in **Taking Off** went further — Lyn Carlyn, a mother on and off the set, was asked to wear street clothes and could not use makeup.

Commenting on his own methods and the phenomenon of European filmmakers interpreting America (4.8), Forman agreed that he was an *auteur* director:

"If I don't want to be modest, I must say — yes. I think that people who write and direct a film are its real authors, but I must admit that to do so, you must obtain a certain kind of confidence from those above you, the producers and the company, and very important help from the people who work with you. I'm very dependent on this confidence from the top, and this help from below. You can be an *auteur*, but if you don't have this understanding from the people who are financing your projects, and if you don't get enough intelligent help from the actors and the crew, then you can be a genius, and your film will not be a personal creation. The way you work demands great intelligence and flexibility from the people you are working with — without that, you're just beating your head against the wall . . .

"This is very important in casting. As I didn't know many actors in New York, readings were arranged. I would have two or three very good possibilities for a part, the first and second better than the third one — but, when I felt the third one more flexible and more in harmony with what my way of thinking and working is, I'd rather cast the third, even if the first and second were better actors.

"If this film is a success, I give a lot of the credit to Buck Henry, who plays a major role. Not only is he an extraordinary actor, but at the same time his attitude and presence on the set help beyond what he brings to the screen. He was of enormous help to me, very cooperative and very sensitive to everything. Nothing was arranged, we didn't talk about these things. But, for example, it is very exhausting for me to work in the English language because it's not my own, and I have to translate everything into Czech, then into English, and I'd always feel uncertain. This was very exhausting, so it very often happened in the afternoon, after lunch, I was down. So a bad, tired atmosphere started to spread around on the set, which was very dangerous.

Teenager Linnea Heacock in rock singers audition in New York City's East Village.

"In that moment, without asking, Buck Henry seemed to sense this danger, and suddenly always mobilized his energies to say something funny to one person, or do something to another person, and suddenly I felt he was keeping the atmosphere I needed to work — and we never even talked about it, I don't know if he was doing it consciously or unconsciously, or if that's his nature . . . incredible talent! In my opinion so important for good results in everything . .

"I think the practical effect (of Europeans' American films) will depend on the success of these films. If more of these American films made by European directors will flop, the companies will very quickly abandon the experiment.

"If some are successful, the European approach and thinking will have a certain impact. I think that it's not the influence of the culture on one part of the world on another part of the world. It's going on anyway, whether people work here or not. I think what's going on in the American cinema today is a little influenced by the European cinema of the last ten years. If you speak of *auteur* cinema, and more and more American filmmakers being free to be *auteurs*, I believe this is the result of the success of *auteur*-type films coming here from Europe five, six, even ten years ago."

Two bright-faced little girls, dressed in stars and stripes, skip to the mike and stop with a jump. Trusting eyes, long curly hair. They pipe away: "Time was once upon, for we, to fly, away — " They stand a moment, skip off . . .

To bright titles rotating, sliding, turning on invisible surfaces a hard-voiced, earnest twentyish blonde wails to electronic guitar chords: "I — I — believe-in, believe-in, believe-in, believe-in — love, love, love-love-love . . . "

A too-bright, too-cool doctor's office. A bald, mournful-looking medic with a bright pink-and-green bowtie faces a man whose own incipient bald spot is innocuous, but undeniable. The slow, redundant voice tells him to imagine he's floating: "You may feel sometimes a magnetic pull . . . "

The girl's guitar thrums; an instant of straight-haired blonde.

The patient is a harassed-looking, perhaps bashful middleager, Larry Tyne (Buck Henry). He's trying very hard. The doctor wants him to meditate. Will he keep on smoking? If living is still exciting.

The Berkeley-type, moaning, chording . . .

The doctor's recorder tells the dangers of smoking. The earnest girl, strumming and asking about love, pops on and off the screen.

Tyne is to make "a fist, with the hand itself." Then, as his eyes roll up "in private," control will return. Earnestly, he rolls them . . .

Cut to more young girls. It's an open audition for singers. A pair bleat: everybody needs happiness, everybody needs love. The organ harmonicas after. A breathless young girl says she's an acrobat too, handstands, begins "Tammy," but her voice cracks on the second line. A bored-looking youth thumbs her off . . .

From a dark corridor emerges a fifteen-year-old, silent-scared, with large, expressive downcast eyes: Jeanie Tyne. We see the dozens of girls standing around, the attractiveness and energy of young bodies and faces, but also dubious and empty expressions. They scan her skeptically. She joins them . . .

A phone rings in suburbia. Mrs. Lynne Tyne is calling another distraught suburban type. Has she heard from their girls? No, the woman's daughter is home, not in the city with Jeanie . . .

A round, stoned-looking girl talks with Jeanie in slow bursts: "The girls in the balcony . . . are all throwing up (snort) . . . they had coke . . . "

Another "intense" girl is on, kicking, strumming: "losing ground — paying the cost, — thinks she's dying . . . "

At a long portable table, the audition judges, youth-culture types, sprawl and slouch and stare dubiously over a mess of papers and Cokes.

Another personality kid bops and bounces, says she's just standin', waitin' and a waitin' —

It's Jeanie's turn. The black organist, who's seen 'em all, gives her a cheery vibrating calliope cue:

Jeanie's mouth opens, but no sound.

A second chance. No sound.

"I'm sorry," Jeanie whispers. "Can I come back?"

An aggressive girl replaces her, belts out: *THE PARTY'S ENDING-*

The next song is the sweet "Let's Get a Little Sentimental." The beat is unbroken throughout, but each line is cut with a different glowing girl singing: freckled and bright-eyed, black elegance in a white gown, fine boned-dark-haired-witchy-intensity; a bouquet of proud, shy, lovely, plain girls' faces, all on the eager trembling edge of womanhood: beautiful, wordless, eerie:

*"Let's start holding hands . . .*
*"Let's start making plans . . . "*

On the second verse, the cuts are all on their slips of notes or memory; shyness, embarrassment, swift touching intimate instants. . .

In the suburbs, the Tynes bicker nervously while another couple watches. The phone rings . . . but there's just breathing, no voice. "Will you speak freely?" Larry Tyne yelps . . .

On the stage, a very young girl begins a slow breathless ballad about her childhood: "Even the Horses Had Wings." For the first time, the other girls are watching, silent . . .

To the hushed young voice the Tynes and their friends enter the girl's neat, somehow abandoned bedroom: shelves of little ceramic and furry animals, one half-smoked cigarette under the bed, strange, simple, stylized drawings in looping, thin pencil lines of flowers, animals, people.

In the silence the girl whispers:
*That was the world*
*When I was a child*
*But it can't be me that's changed,*
*It's got to be the world.*

In the silence, the adults decide without speaking to return to their high-ceilinged living room, with knotty pine panelling, doilies on the TV and piano, an odd "perspective painting" . . .

At the audition, the fat girl begins to speak even less coherently. She's on Mighty Quinn, and it feels s-o g-o-o-d. She giggles, sighs, then struggles. On the stage, a girl slowly sings "Long Term Medical Effects." They're not yet known so she's just gonna get stoned. In the crowd, the fat girl grunts and struggles, freaking out, against those holding her . . .

At home, a petulant Larry Tyne says he wouldn't know where to *begin* to look; "But we're just *sitting* here — if she *needs* us — ," wails Lynne.

Woebegotten: "The point is — but *where* needing us?"

A mischievous-looking girl strums "Ode to a Screw," a madrigal in which, in an ethereal voice, she offers the Russians, English, king, queen and uglies to her boyfriend. *"But before you fuck them — darling, you must fuck me!"* The other girls look upset . . .

Pan of a twelve-foot police bulletin board with masses of notices and snapshots of kids. A big portrait of a smiling Jeanie, in soft browns, incongruously dominates it. "We're at the station now," Larry Tyne rasps on the phone. "They don't know. They've given us the name of some bar" . . .

On the couch at home, Mrs. Tyne sits distraught beside Margot (Linnea Hancock), a matron with short blonde curls. She puts down the phone and smiles. Feeling disoriented and kittenish, the two women are suddenly intimate: "*Twice*? You're crazy! I can't even get undressed — and he goes — I was going to — he came in."

The women giggle over their drinks. It's the hour of midnight confidences: "You want to know what happened?" The little blonde rushes. "He woke me up in the middle of the night, he told me to get out of bed, and wanted me to — sing — ."

"Sing?"

Sing. And to dance. Forget the neighbors. So she danced . . . what?

Flushed, embarrassed, she won't tell . . .

In the smoky bar, between undershirted men around a pool table

From the motion picture "TAKING OFF" (Universal, 1971). Courtesy of Universal Pictures.

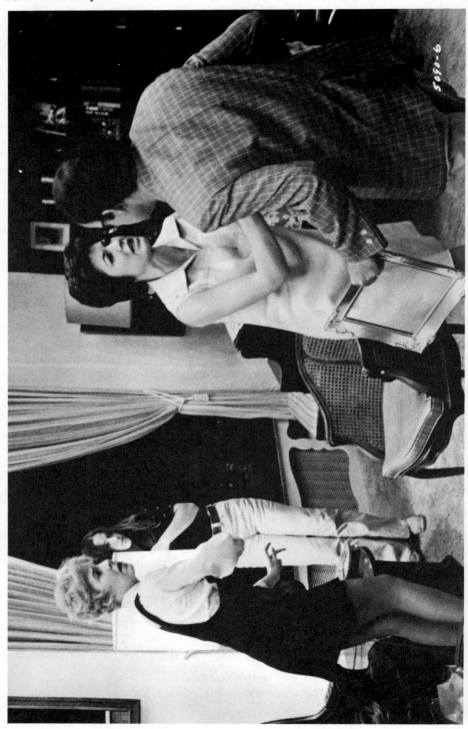

Lynn Carlin urges irate husband Buck Henry to control himself as daughter Linnea Heacock hides, and friend Georgia Engel tries to help.

and a dignified matron who has brought her cat, Larry Tyne rolls his eyes, raises his fist: "I need my body to live. I owe my body protection . . ."

At home, the little blonde housewife, arms waving from hips dances from side to side, kicking to right and left: "Bet ma money on a bob-tailed nag, do-dah!" she sings, dreamy-gay. "Oh, they run all day . . . a-a-and they run all night . . ."

Lynn Tyne looks on in wonder . . .

In the dim bar, the pool balls click. Larry Tyne, drunk on his barstool, practices the trance, then watches in beady-eyed helplessness as a half-eaten hardboiled egg rolls off the bar. He starts to peel another, bites, dreamily spits shell. The two men reel toward the door . . .

At home, Mrs. Tyne kneels before a speechless Jeanie: "What did you take? Did you smoke? What? I'm not mad at you, I just have to know — "

Dreamy-eyed, the teenager shakes her head silently.

In lurches Larry Tyne: *"Where were you?"* he hoarses, leaning on the doorframe, charging clumsily. Lynn struggles with him.

"I'm drunk, and I'm going to hit her!"

In stumbles his trotters-fetishist companion, delighted: "You found her!"

Mrs. Tyne rushes to the phone. But the family doctor has gone back to sleep beside the receiver: "That's strange, now I hear breathing."

Suddenly, all feel the emptiness. The four run into the lane behind the house. In the morning, the wind rushes in the grass. To discordant Dvorak we see quiet green lawns before modest homes, cars whispering by, a man walking his dog. But Jeanie is gone again . . .

The city is nailed beneath the summer sun by the Empire State Building. A green bus wheezes poison, passes to reveal Larry Tyne searching wearily. The Village: brightly-painted windows, psychedelic-chalk rainbows on bricks, strange skinny private boys and girls. On the sidewalk, Larry Tyne eyes one dynamite chick. In the park, he raises his fist, rolls his eyes. A passing black raises his own in answer.

A harassed, sweating Larry Tyne in a candy store shoves Jeanie's snapshot at the whitehaired, immigrant proprietress: "It's my daughter."

"No, no," squawks the old woman.

Impatiently, he makes her put it in a cigar box with some others, picks one up. This girl is in a back booth with three roughs, sweet-faced with glasses and long red hair. Look!

"Go, go, just leave me alone," wails the lady. She backs away.

"Hey," Tyne says sourly, "What about my — you, hey! — "

The old lady shakes her head. "I don't know . . . I don' wanna tell you nothin' . . . "

Tyne shoves into a phone booth and calls the runaway's home: "She's sitting right here — "

But no, she's getting up with three strutting, bearded, filthy-jeaned, booted characters. Hell's Angels. Tyne doesn't hesitate: "Can I ask you a question?"

Neither do the Angels: "Hey, *creep*! You're bothering her. . . "

No, no, he just wants — the girl is silent. It just so happens this girl is a missing person — Nancy Lockston! A guitar starts beating. The girl gasps, spins, flees outside as the Angels close in —

More guitar. A matron in a lacey crocheted white blouse bursts from a braking taxi, waving and screaming —

The unpaid driver is right behind her. "Hey, *lady* — "

The girl goes past a block of tenements with a long-legged lope, her mother clocking behind her.

Onstage, to the thrumming guitar, a bitter-sweet girl croons the sardonic "Lessons in Love Are Free" as Larry Tyne backs away from the three aroused psychopaths along the shabby crowded street.

*"Oh, lessons in love are free, said he —*
*Lessons in love are free — "*

Tyne slows down to a waddle, casting citizen-type looks. But the Angels keep on coming —

*"So he took me by the hand —*
*He showed me where to stand — "*

Tyne turns and sprints around a corner. The girl's mother comes down the block towards him, looking lost. Tyne peeks back over his shoulder. With a roar, two Angels appear on their cycles. The third waves from the hijacked cab. The guitar flourishes:

*"And said — lessons in love are free."*

In an empty, noonday expresso shop, Mrs. Lockston gushes her thanks. Lynn comforts her: Jeanie has been gone a week.

"Oh, mine's been gone ten months."

But Mrs. Lockston, with a penetrating smile, feels you should get out of it what you can — it's a life experience. For a moment, we see a nude girl sawing at a violin. Looking has brought them closer together. If Larry and her could look . . .

Tyne smiles uneasily, calls his wife.

A wail: "Get back. She's been arrested for shoplifting. She's in jail. Three hundred miles away!!!"

The Tynes hurry north by car "A Japanese portable TV set." "Sony?" "Mitsubishi."

A sweating, hulking, apologetic-faced cop leads them into a squad room. A dark-skinned young girl sits in a corner.

"Oh, no, that's Corinne Divito."

The cop assures her it's Jeanne Tyne . . . After a while, he comes out again. The girl is Corinne, and knows nothing of Jeanie. "Sorry it had to happen . . . if you'd like coffee?"

Big cars rushing through the twilight, constellations of red and white lights. Lynn's voice wails: "Anything but shoplifting . . . and when it wasn't Jeanie . . . "

An aggravated Larry Tyne declares that she's off having a terrific time with her friends. We should have as much fun, goddamn it! . . .

A loud, violent guitar vibrates. On a narrow stage, Tina Turner springs forward like a lioness in heat, twisting sensuously in the spotlight, dark eyes flashing, tawny mane flying. The band plays rock feverishly, and now three lovely black girls in silver join her in a frenzied rhythm. But beyond the blazing group, the club is full of gray, lined faces.

"Another gin on the rocks!" Lynn Tyne calls. Larry cancels the order. In the foreground, an ancient couple twostep to the galvanic rock.

"Just the check," Tyne hearties. "We have a four-hour drive . . ."

But if he's very tired, Lynn soothes, why can't they stay the night. Her hand clamps his knee. The music twangs!

"Look," he blusters, "let's go to sleep. I can't do this kind of dance."

"You're not looking at me — not *seeing* me," she tells him, and proves it with her hand. Tyne yips!

Grouchy, he slinks off to bed. "If you wanna come on, come on. If you wanna stay, stay!"

A fat, glib fellow slides into the empty seat, his beaky one-expression pal takes the third. "My name is Norman — how are ya? My friend Skyler."

The two are tedious: Norman idiotic, Skyler bleakly disinterested. Lynn slides out of her seat "to go the little girl's room."

Idiotically, Skyler urges: "Go after her, man, she wants ya!"

Lynn stumbles down the hotel corridor, slipping off her shoes.

The satchel-fannied Norman waddles grotesquely after, his pants half down, easing open the door to her dark room.

Tyne, alone in bed, switches on the light.

Flustered, drunk, pants at half mast, Norman beats a clumsy retreat . . .

In their suite, Lynn comes out of the bathroom with a secret smile. In her nightgown she prances before the mirror: "Bet my money on a bob-tailed nag — somebody bet on — on — the bay!"

Cut: A blacktie crowd cheers.

Cut: A tough Larry Tyne: "Do you want to come to bed?"
"Yes I do!"

Cut: The Blacktie crowd: dark suits and evening gowns. They're in a large hotel hall, the kind of room rented for banquets and receptions. A man at a podium waits for quiet, over his head the banner: SOCIETY FOR THE PARENTS OF FUGITIVE CHILDREN. He gestures to a smirking girl with long brown weeping-willow hair that hides her face. "We have with us tonight Miss Ellen Lubar — away six months — who may have seen your children, and will be happy to answer your questions. If you will form a line . . . "

The adults, mostly middle-aged couples with careworn expressions, line up awkwardly. Each has a photograph of his runaway in a plastic envelope pinned to label or bodice. The girl peers at one man's picture: "I think I know her . . . "

"That's my son," the man murmurs.

Someone's waving at the Tynes. It's Mrs. Lockston with her husband, Ben, a foolish-looking overdressed Dr. Zhivago with a big nose. "Hello," she brays, "How are you?" . . .

Through the silent home, Jeanne wanders, calling out softly for her parents. She is unchanged, except for her jeans which have been hacked off at the knee . . .

At the S.P.F.C. meeting, Ben Lockston, the S.P.F.C. president, declares that they not only seek their children, they also seek to understand them — what pressures them into taking drugs. But to really understand, they must have similar experiences. Hence, he proposes they conduct an illegal experiment, for there are considerations which transcend legalities . . .

He takes a breath: "That is why this marijuana, which I am told is particularly pure in form, and therefore particularly pure as to reaction, is what I propose you indulge in with me tonight."

A beanpole young man with a great frizzy globe of hair, granny glasses, hippie attire, and a mournfully sardonic air faces a group of the well-dressed adults in a plush lounge decorated with American Gothic paintings. He's Mr. Evans, a patient of a psychiatrist-member. "All right," he crisply tells them, holding a clumsily-made cigarette. "This is a joint. Take a joint, with the open end facing you — "

He goes on with his pot-smoking drill: inhale very deeply, hold for a count of ten. The group, all furs, heavy makeup, stiff hairdos, tuxedos and dark suits, practice: balding, worry-lined execs compare joints, matrons in falls and rhinestone glasses finger them nervously.

"Do not, repeat, do not, hold onto the joint," Vincent insists. "This is called *Bogarting* the joint, and is very rude. Keep passing till the joint is very small — I will collect those. Questions?"

A hornrimmed exec: "You said count to ten. How fast?"

A gray PTA-president: "Do dope and alcohol mix?"

"Oh, they'll mix," Vincent smiles. "Now we're ready to light up."

The S.P.F.C. begin puffing nervously. At once, a pudgy woman

From the motion picture "TAKING OFF" (Universal, 1971). Courtesy of Universal Pictures.

Parents experiment with marijuana — Buck Henry, Lynn Carlin, Audra Lindley, Paul Benedict.

in magenta begins to cough and giggle. The habitually concerned, now apprehensive, guilty yet expectant mature faces are cut against the grim, disapproving portraits of Kansas pioneer couples and New London widows with tight-bunned hair.

"Inhale — now pass the joint — !" Vincent calls.

Some are counting, a few ladies already giggling. Larry Tyne puffs away. "Hey, mister — no Bogarting!"

Clouds of smoke rise, and Vincent puts on a slow, piping record of head music. Some execs are getting nothing: "Smells like stinkweed to me." Others giggle and pass it on. Vincent sings with the music, moving around with palms up:

Fly . . . fly . . . fly like a big bird
Can't you feel . . . feel your whole body flying away?

The lawyer, in level tones, says he's beginning to feel something. On the walls, crochety old ancestors condemn the happy crew of careworn adults. A big jelly of a woman dances around, puts her head on the smiling hippie's chest: "Go with it. Don't think — just take the impulse." He waves his arms.

President Ben is standing, palms together, looking very pleased. Some sing along with the record, dance, stare about with bemused expressions through the clouds of smoke, try to appear high. A woman laughs shrilly.

One skeptic, cheated: "I don't feel anything." . . .

The Tynes with the Lockstons, laughing, wander into their home: "Oh, what a beautiful house . . . "

Larry Tyne gestures at his bottle collection, then swoops behind the bar for full ones. They all wander about the room, talking, laughing. Ben peers at the "perspective painting," painted vertical corregations like the side of an accordion that show a clipper ship, a Victorian lady, or a bouquet, depending on where you stand.

"That's remarkable!" Ben announces solemnly: "That's what I mean by a work of art."

They all burst out laughing . . .

Around the big coffee table, the giggling, formally dressed adults watch Ben Lockston, glitter-eyed, pull out a deck: "We are going to play — we are going, to play, this is — Texas One Card Showdown!"

"I'm not ready," Larry Tyne says, and slugs down a drink.

Nobody knows how to play.

Ben leers: "Everybody's supposed to take one card and — low man the loser!"

"Ready, ready!" sings Lynn over silly laughter.

The cards go down. She loses: "Okay!"

"Okay, what?"

"Okay, you gotta take something off — "

She stares at them amiably: "I did, I did — my shoes!" One in each hand, she waves them, thosses them behind her back.

"Ha-ha-ha-ha-ha-"

The games goes on . . .

To applause, Ben Lockston removes his jacket. Straight-faced, Anne Lockston claps.

The rehearsal organ begins chording richly: "He's Got the Whole World in His Hands." The four clap, giggle, snap their fingers. Larry Tyne loosens his jacket as the others laugh and screech.

*He's got you and me, brothers, in his hands —*
*He's got everybody —*

To wild laughter, Larry Tyne is forced out of his trousers. A moment later he holds up his shorts, then flings them away.

But now his face is pathetically upset as Lynn leans forward to unhook her bra, crouching over the table as she plays the next round.

"It's bad for your spine to sit that way," Ben proscribes. So she plays with her arms crossed in front . . .

Upstairs, the shouts and burst of laughter have wakened Jeanie, who wraithlike, moves towards the little veranda above the living room.

Below, Ben Lockston and his wife, suspiciously well-dressed, sprawl back in their chairs along with a cringing but laughing Lynn. Standing on the table, naked as a jaybird, hands over his privates, violin record in the background, Larry Tyne is paying his last forfeit with an aria: "La-LA-LA-la-la-lalala!"

His daughter watches, hand to mouth. The others swivel to see her. Then, all below is fumbling, self-conscious confusion as Ben Lockston rumbles: "Uh, humm, I think we should all be going — " The violin continues softly. Larry keeps falling down trying to get into his pants, then pulls and pulls at a shirt cuff with the button already done. "I don't know what to say," they call emptily at their daughter. With more cheer: "It's really amazing — the way marijuana affects — " The Tynes stumble through their goodbyes, then Larry forces on the rest of his clothes, tossing his wife her bra, buttoning it: "I've got to talk to her." Lynn Tyne puts her face in her hands, cries.

In the girl's bedroom, she is silent still as Larry, with great patience, gets nods for we were worried, you were with a boy, do we know him, I think we should meet him.

Quietly: "Your mother and I would like to meet him. Now you invite him to dinner, and if he's not a coward, he'll come" . . .

Jeanie, in a green sheath, answers the door: "This is Jamie."

Jamie, a skinny nineteen with long black beard and hair, a peace symbol on chair on his flowered white silk shirt, comes in.

Like Jeanie, he hardly speaks at dinner, his eyes always darting

From the motion picture "TAKING OFF" (Universal, 1971). Courtesy of Universal Pictures.

Teenager Linnea Heacock brings musician David Gittler to meet her dismayed parents.

away. Mr. Tyne: "Uh, you're a musician."

Jeanie explains: "Organ, bass and piano . . . and he sings."

Make any money at it?

Last year: $290,000.

Mr. Tyne sputters into his wine. In an instant he's puffing furiously away.

"Before taxes," the boy goes on. "You see a lot of things you kind of go against, you kind of hate — so you write some songs about them . . . then you end up paying for the same things."

"Maybe after dinner you'll sing something for us," Tyne asks.

Jamie is dubious: "I don't know if I could get my rocks off . . . "

On the carpet, Jamie and Jeanie sit silent together, looking blank and a little skeptical. Up above, Larry Tyne stands beside the piano as his wife plays, celebrating in song:

*Take my hand, I'm a stranger in paradise*
*All lost in a wonderland, a stranger in paradise*
*If I stand starry-eyed, there's a danger in paradise*
*For mortals who stand beside, an angel like you —*

To the same fast hard strumming guitar as the start, the closing credits appear . . .

Forman is reluctant, for several reasons to discuss the interpretation and implications of **Taking Off** as social comment. He told me (4.8) that in any case he did not base his films on political or philosophical premises, though he does not disapprove in principle of those who do: "It's just not my cup of tea." He would rather leave the meanings to the reviewers and aesthetes. Finally, he added, he feels it is improper for a guest to be critical of his host, especially a very new guest.

At other times, Forman has spoken of **Taking Off** in larger contexts. Speaking about the making of the film (4.11), Forman summed it up as "something that is inherently sad and present its other side; that is, to show that it can also be funny. In doing this, I always try to catch my people, through the lens of the camera, as they really are. When I succeed in doing this, I am very happy and the work becomes a part of my life." He has said that he likes making comedies because he likes going to them, and was inspired by the great silent American comedians he saw in the 1940s. Larry Tyne, to one reviewer, resembles a cross between Harold Lloyd and Jack Lemmon, the archetypical neurotic American male in a squeeze.

In one early interview (4.15), Forman did discuss runaways in America and Czechoslovakia:

"The majority of runaway kids do really boring things — the great thing for them is that they ran away. They can sit for days in a friend's apartment looking up at the ceiling and smoking pot. It's the parents who are put into action — it's a long-term crisis that's put into the open. The parents make a better topic — their situation is tragic, and that's good for comedy.

"There is the same tension [in Czechoslovakia], but it's harder to run away. The biggest city is Prague, but it's easy for the police to find a kid among one million people. There is also a shortage of apartments — there's nowhere to go. No 18-year-old has his own place.

"I met seven or eight families with kids who had returned home. I was surprised that I liked them all — you couldn't say the kids or the parents were right. There was no drunk father who beat the mother — it was interesting because it was puzzling.

"Today, anything you do in films realistically has political results, because you are describing reality. There is no political message in my work — I do stories about people. When I'm finished, the critics can look at them from a social or political view. I don't have to put in political meanings before hand. They were there automatically, whether you want it or not."

The critical response to **Taking Off** was uniformly favorable, but few discussed the film with great seriousness. Vincent Canby (4.2) said "**Taking Off** is not a major movie experience, but it is — a good deal of the time — a charming one." Canby saw it as Forman's specialty: a tender farce played out in very bleak circumstances, though with affection for everybody. He does note the songs as commentary, and the endless young faces which seriously, comically, "surround the film."

Molly Haskell (4.6) saw the film as a journey for the distraught parents: desperation, distraction, diversion, and a final new desperation (the strip poker). That they go on as normal next day makes **Taking Off** the mortification of the middle class. The film can seem cruel because it is about auditions: "He catches characters in moments of exposure and humiliation, in expressions of emotional nakedness next to which physical nakedness would be a merciful distraction. He has an unerring instinct for finding faces — . . . and capturing that moment in which hope and disappointment, youth and age intersect for one absurd and agonizing instant. Forman is a director of comic vignettes, a limited for vastly underrated form."

Penelope Gilliatt (4.5) would agree that the film is a comedy of manners, though much warmer: "Forman sees privileged human beings as having an instinct to continue that is fortunate for the life term of the species but ill conceived for their own comfort, and he makes the observation in a style of charred comedy that is very Slavic . . . The parents in **Taking Off** have been programmed all their lives to dress up in black tie and sequins and to look as if they were enjoying themselves when a hundred of them are gathered together. So when the function happens to be a horribly unhappy meeting of parents whose children have run away, the grief is hidden and the rules are served . . . the parents, crippled by politeness and fake office bonhomie and high heels, recover whatever rusting scraps of force and grown-up love they can from the wreck of their age group's self-esteem . . . having to grapple with a secret diffidence. The runaway's mother is delicately hipped on modesty in the middle of the strip poker romp: it is a sweet performance longing for fun, prudish mostly for her husband's sake."

One dissatisfied commentator was Robert Hatch (4.7), who felt that the young people were assumed sympathetic, the middle-aged middle-class made foolish for a laugh: "Forman finds endearing the ebullience of the uncomely, untalented, ill–coordinated and no longer young. The spectacle of a fat and foolish matron dancing solo to her singing of "Camptown Races" is less characteristic of American mores than of Forman's preoccupations." Hatch thinks Forman correctly sees the generation gap as a matter of age, the young preferring their own tribe, but thinks the Czech insists on treating everything as a huge joke.

For myself the comic aspects of **Taking Off** are successful secondary qualities to an eerie but fascinating major theme: a mostly visual essay on youth's essence, woven from the songs, the brief shots of the aspiring girls, and the comic baseline of the parent's quest. Forman's scripting and direction of the adults shows the terrible weight of adult behavior the parents must drag around – they are forced to always appear like the ideal couples wanted by the producers of 1950s television – "happy people with happy problems." Lynn Tyne is always cheerful but insecure, Larry Tyne forces himself to be cool and rational but keeps slipping; getting drunk, swinging at his daughter, wanting to have fun himself but stomping off to bed.

Contrasted with them are the young people. At the very start of the film, the harrassed father is asked if living is exciting? His response: a Berkeley blonde singing of love. And just as the adults are shown in "their medium," situation comedy, the young people appear singing their own songs, written by themselves.

Unlike the adults, Forman does not dwell on any routine or patterned responses for the youngsters. What he shows is their wordless closeness to the mysteries of life and childhood itself, which are somehow lost as we grow older. Thus, the young people pay attention only to the breathless "Even the Horses Had Wings," and the small empty room with its little animals and bizarre drawings discomforts all the adults.

Youth itself, its sensitivity, hope and potentials, are shown raw in the dozens of faces which "surround" the film. Like Jeanie Tyne, the youngsters seem to prefer their own sweet music, or merely silence, to the adults' weary speech full of rationalizations, muddle, or new confusions.

The popular adult cliche-paradoxes of youth are joked away: a girl sings "Long Term Physical Effects Are Not Yet Known" while another girl casually "freaks out" — both facts simply acknowledged. When Larry Tyne goes after the Lockston girl, his naivete is the joke of a TV comedy father, contrasted with the wise "Lessons in Love Are Free." But the girl herself, and the Hell's Angels for that matter, are neither innocent or hypocritical as far as can be seen. Like Jeanie Tyne, Forman gives them the privacy youth chooses for itself.

The final scene between all the Tynes and Jamie brings the theme to its conclusion: Jamie, with a single number — $290,000 — would appear to have answered all possible complaints of the parents about his relationship with their daughter. The adult world intrudes just once more in the taxes he pays — which go to make the things he hates — a contradiction, like living in hypocrisy and innocence, something youth simply must get away from. In the end, Mr. Tyne seems to begin to acknowledge their strange ways: a stranger in paradise.

No critic has attacked **Taking Off** as a romanticization of the world of runaways: no hard drugs, no venereal disease, no pathological people, no nasty adults. It is, of course, stylized comedy. But in its thematic treatment of youth and age, it is the most consistent. It leaves out a fake "counter-culture" and a revolution that doesn't exist, contrasting only the things each generation claims as its own, showing the essences of two ways of living, two modes of thought.

## Jean-Luc Godard

# MADE IN U.S.A.

**Made in U.S.A.** began when Georges de Bourelard, one of Godard's old producers, approached him to make a simple story film, cheaply and quickly, "as only you can," to help him out of some financial difficulties. Godard was making **Two or Three Things I Know about Her** at the time, but thought the idea of making two films at once posed a unique sort of challenge, as well as the opportunity to help out an old friend.

The project apparently had a violent and complex metamorphosis. In a statement made in 1966, Godard said he wanted to remake John Huston's **The Big Sleep**, which he had just seen again, with Anna Karina taking the Humphrey Bogart role, and the story connected to the Ben Barka Affair, with Karina trying to unravel some impenetrable mystery. The Ben Barka Affair was something of a mystery itself: the kidnapping and possible murder of that Left Wing journalist while arranging an international conference, possibly with police compliance and even C.I.A. intervention. Georges Fignon, a specialist in underworld films, knew Barka's whereabouts until he disappeared, and subsequently also vanished. In Godard's early script, Fignon flees to the provinces, writes his fiancee to join him, but she arrives to find him dead. The Fignon character, called Politzer, has died for no apparent reason, and Karina sets out to discover his past. Soon enough she is trapped in a network of political intrigue, and winds up writing an article about it.

An eighteen-page scenario Godard prepared to raise money for the film is similar. Called "The Secret," it makes Karina a girl from a small town, whose lover dies under mysterious circumstances, and who encounters three or four people desperate to discover some terrible secret that he held. In some ways, this second scenario resembles Mickey Spillane's *Kiss Me Deadly*.

This final, abbreviated treatment retains something of the first plots, but is most notable for its highly stylized, experimental form, including many of Godard's narrative-destroying devices like the simultaneous monologues, plot connections off-handedly dropped, sudden shifts in tone, "quotes." Two notable conceits are the sounds which always hide the full name of Richard Po-, and the deliberately garbled, painfully loud, almost enraging tapes of his voice. Further confusing things are the allusions to the Kennedy assassination as well as the Ben Barka Affair, together with the intense beauty of Coutard's color cinematography, and Karina herself.

The lovely brunette Paula Nelson asleep, on her breast a crime novel: *Goodbye Life, Goodbye Love*. She opens her eyes: "Happiness, for instance . . . whenever he wanted something, so did I. Or fame, for him . . . he only had to say what he wanted. When he didn't want anything, neither did I . . . I only wanted what I knew he wanted." She is wearing a turquoise dress with bold diagonal stripes.

A maid enters with whiskey, changes the towels. Paula wanders to the window. Outside, Widmark and Aldrich, two cool executive types in a black Citroen. Paula paces restlessly: "How many people are there in Atlantic City?"

She looks out again. The two men in the car wait, unmoving.

At a knock, Paula takes a pistol from a false cookbook, slits the door, then tries to shut it. A foreign accented voice: "Attractive as ever, Mademoiselle Nelson . . . There are one or two things I want to talk to you about . . . !"

The speaker pushes his way in, a gangster-type in Panama hat, but very short, perhaps to Paula's armpits. She frisks him, pushes him down on the bed: "Talk!"

"The Moroccan war seems to have turned you nasty," he cuts.

Paula regards herself in the bathroom mirror, drinks some whiskey.

The tough, named Typhus, murmurs: "War is never over. Trafalgar, Sudan, Leningrad, Berlin, Hanoi . . . it changes its name, but it's always the same . . . What are you doing here?"

Paula half-playfully pulls his hat down over his eyes: "What do you want, you lousy bastard? What did Richard die of?"

Typhus doesn't know. He read *Quest France*, then came over pronto.

Paula twirls the revolver, aims. Typhus flinches, then smooths his hair: "I only arrived, saw you come in, asked the number of the room so I could take one next door. Why don't we work together?"

We see Paula's face alone: "I don't know a thing. He just sent me a telegram, we were hardly seeing each other. I don't know if I still love him, but I owed him for what was between us. They told me he'd been taken to the hospital in the fifth region." She toys with her hair to a jet's sound overhead. Tersely: "Tell me something I don't know."

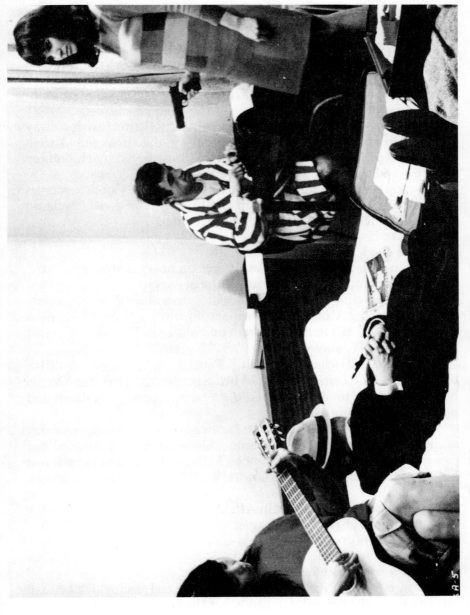

Paula Nelson (Anna Karina) confronts "Typhus," bitterly asking after her lost love.

"You know quite well it's a secret."

Paula, intense: "What secret?"

"There's no need to start that again . . . there must be some pretty frightened people in Paris, in the Ministry of Information, the Interior — even in the Government — supposing we work together, then split 50-50."

"Yes, all right, okay." She takes two shoes from her wardrobe. "Which goes best with this dress, the white or the blue?"

She suddenly strikes him on the temple with the blue shoe's heel, making a bloody wound, then drags him into the next room, past a wardrobe holding a Beethoven t-shirt, dumps him on the bed. A search yields toothpaste and brush, *La Quinzaine Litteraire*. Closeup: scrawled in red: Dr. Samuel Korvo, autopsy, and an address.

Godard's soft voice comments: "Already fiction carries away reality. Already there is blood and mystery in the air, already I seem to be plunged into a film by Walt Disney, but played by Humphrey Bogart — and therefore a political film."

A goodhumored, impudent soul named David Goodis emerges from the bath, Paula covering him. He types one-fingered. Paula on the windowsill. "What's she done to Uncle Edgar?"

"You're his nephew?"

"Is he dead?"

"No, no, Paula explains, "I'm the person he wanted to speak to." In the bathroom, she finds a beautiful Japanese girl.

"She's the girl I love," David declares. In a closeup, the Japanese beauty sings in a strange language, accompanying herself on guitar.

"She's Doris Misoguchi. We were on holiday in Paris, Uncle Edgar had invited us. We stayed exactly . . . 127 years."

"Hmmm, just what I thought," Paula says. "But you can't see her very often?" Doris sits on the bed, strumming her guitar. On the bed, Paula picks up *La Quinzaine Litteraire*, tears off the front and puts it away.

Goodis goes on. "She lives too far away. I only saw her every day at breakfast, at lunchtime, at teatime. She lived at Levallois, and had to get a visa every time she came to Paris . . . I only saw her the rest of the time, that is to say not at breakfast, lunchtime, teatime, dinnertime."

"And what are you doing in Atlantic City?"

David stares at the typing paper. We read:

*In this mirror I am enclosed alive*
*and true like we think angels*
*and not like reflections are*

David is writing a novel which will never end, and which he shall call the unfinished novel. He hands her the latest sheet, and in close-up she reads it accompanied by the guitar:

*Who then can explain this feeling of a long pain?*
*And my life and the world, and who would ever believe in it?*
*She only loved what passes, and I was the color of time*

Paula finishes the page, gets up and prepares to leave: "When he gets up, tell him I've disappeared." . . . A jet roars over.

Outside, she passes a vivid red, white and blue poster. An emphatic Beethoven piano trio sounds, followed by two chords, the strings prolonged: BANG, BANGgggggg

Paula is inside against a red wall. A girl in a white medical coat enters, Paula against the wall swinging her hair in luscious arabesques. The girl consults a diary, leaves. Paula, against a turquoise wall, loads a gun and hides it in a hollow *Larousse Cookbook*. In silence, we see her talking to the medical assistant.

Godard, voiceover: "Is it really you whom I shall find dead dear Richard, my king? In what farcical tragedy are you making me play the walk-on?" On the screen, Paula fluffs her hair, rises to drive the assistant into the surgery at gunpoint. A corpse sits in a dentist's chair, with a bloody bandaged head. Paula pulls away the bandages, showing naked eyes and teeth in the flayed skull. As a jet roars over, Paula raises the gun, but a doctor comes up behind her with his own pistol.

Paula sits against the red wall, just as before.

Godard's voice: "Fortunately, I had turned brunette and Professor Korvo didn't recognize the blonde student of Agadir."

Longshot: Neon signs, glowing brilliantly in the night. Traffic sounds. Marianne Faithful begins "As Tears Go By": "It is the evening of the day — "

Paula sits at a formica table. The barman comes over with a drink: "You don't look too cheerful. Haven't you found anything out yet?" The barman serves a workman, then returns to Paula with a bottle: "Call me barman or Paul, it's easier."

She plays number riddles with him: ("During the war, 70 plus 14 was 40"), then joins the two at the bar. The barman asks the workman to count everything there. But what's a bar?

"Well, a bar is . . . it's a place, I mean a room . . . that is, it's several people gathered together under the gaze of a barman, and then it's also a room where liquids are poured out. In fact, it's both at once."

The workman argues a bar can't be two things at once, but agrees to start his count: "I can see a glass, some bottles, a rose, some windows to my right and then a door, which is both in front of me and behind you as well." In the exquisite full color shot, all this is clear.

Barman: "Ah, there you are, a thing can be in two different places at the same time. Carry on."

The workman goes on, Paula walking lackadaisically back and

Paula (Anna Karina) visits bar in which language and communication break down.

forth in front of the bar: "Yes, and there're four walls surrounding the bar, the floor under our feet, and me, Paula, in a desperate situation she doesn't know how to get out of."

The barman tells them they've just made a list of words, and must do something with them.

"If you like, I'll try to show off with sentences, but I don't like doing it," the workman quips. He says sentences are collections of words which make nonsense.

If he won't talk in sentences, the barman won't serve him.

The workman has a try: "The glass is not in my wine. The counter is kicking mademoiselle. He is not what we are . . . "

Donald, still sullen, and Widmark walk past the three to the bar. Paula recognizes the two who had her under surveillance.

The barman: "What'll it be?"

Donald simply takes over the bar, looks at Paula resentfully, serves Widmark a drink, returns to the customer's side, commenting coolly: "If you're asked, you don't know."

Facing the camera, Donald wears a huge: Kiss Me, I'm Italian button. He takes out a jiggle puzzle and plays it.

Cut: A sign: V.O. (i.e., Version Originale, or original version).

An electric newstrip reads: Armed soldiers will protect the candidates in Sunday's elections.

"You could at least say something," Paula tells Donald.

"What is the maximum speed of love?" he quips. "68 kph — one more and you'd be head to tail — ha-ha-ha."

We see Marianne Faithful, the man behind her absorbed in a magazine. "You might least say something," he also complains.

"I'm fed up."

The man goes, and Marianne again sings "As Tears Go By," Paula watching appreciatively. Paula, Widmark and Donald exchange significant glances as the song goes on:

It is the evening of the day
I sit and watch the children play
smiling faces I can see
But not for me
I sit and watch the tears go by
My riches can't buy everything
I want to hear the children sing
all I hear is the sound
of rain falling on the ground
I sit and watch as tears go by
It is the evening of the day
I sit and watch the children play
Doing things I used to do
They think are new
I sit and watch as tears go by.

**93**

In closeup, Paula's profile is shown against a dark background: "Whatever I do I can't escape my responsibility towards another person. My silence acts on him just as my words do. My going away worries him as much as my presence. My indifference may be as fatal to him as my interference. My sometimes thoughtless concern is deadly to him."

In closeup, Paula's reverse profile is tearful: "Either this life is nothing or else it must be everything. By contemplating the possibility of losing it, rather than submitting it to action, I place in the very center of my relative existence an absolute reference: morality."

Closeup of Paula's full face: "In this sense, the absolute is nowhere but here. No past can qualify it, no future event can compromise it. I choose to exist in order to become more present to myself, to Dick, and to others."

A bright light. Four women paddle in an indoor swimming pool as Paula walks past.

Paula walks back the other way as a loudspeaker calls: "Daisy Canyon wanted in Solarium No. 4, Ruby Gentry in Oxygenation Room No. 7."

Two girls in tights exercise with pedal machines and weights. Paula walks past more bored girls on pedal machines. A suited, scholarly man beckons her on, into a white office. Loudspeaker: "Calling Dr. Ludwig."

What Paula says she wants is quite simple: "All I want to know is whether it's true that Dick . . . that Richard Po — (the phone rings) . . . died of a heart attack."

"You're his sister?" The doctor seated with her consults a book: Groddeck's *In the Depths of Man*.

"No, two years ago we were going to get married."

" . . . Look, here's his certificate. There's nothing about it."

Paula pauses: "Yes, even at Treblinka and Auschwitz people ended up dying of a heart attack."

He pauses as the scholarly type enters and whispers, replying "Tell Monsieur Widmark that the person I was thinking of has telephoned."

Paula's face is closeup: "Why was it you they called to certify his death?"

"Because I used to see him often. I'm the president of the club. He was very lonely. I introduced him around."

"Loneliness can hardly be a cause of death," Paula replies.

"I don't understand," the doctor tells her. "You really think there might be a connection between loneliness and an organic illness?" . . .

An exterior garden. To a jet's roar, the scholarly one seeks a number in a little red book, dials a red phone.

Paula's face: "Why are you giving me all these stories. I'm asking for the truth."

"You don't like telling stories? I think you're wrong. Dickens, Melville, Hammet, they're all better than the audio visual methods of true representation."

Paula, fighting: "You didn't attend the mayor. He was killed too. A whole petrol dump went up."

"You're sure he had no family?"

"No. Dick had no one but me. I shall revenge him."

"I don't understand."

With sarcasm: "In that case there's no point in KANT-tinuing our KANT-versation." She turns to go . . .

A red taxi draws up to a turquoise wall. Paula steps out, pays the driver. Donald follows her . . .

Godard, in a soft voiceover: "I quickly realized: everyone wanted to keep this affair hushed up, I was risking my life. But perhaps I would discover something which I could sell to the opposite press afterwards."

Paula walks through a back garden riotous with flowers. She enters a house at the end, comes out, shuts a door to the narrow street, asks the way from someone . . .

Godard: "When I returned for the second time at the end of the afternoon to pick up Richard's things, the weather was fine enough to make a color film. An anonymous caller was to meet me in the garage. I recognized the accent of a typist who had gone off with him."

Paula turns down a narrow alley. An arm reaches out, grabs her.

Comic strip frame: Exclamation points – *bing!*

Paula's face, unconsious on a dirty floor beside a bucket, blue hubcap, red gas can, *Newsweek* under her arms. She stirs: "Where am I? I walk across countries filled with blood. Is life anything but war? Do we ruin life by killing any fewer people?"

Widmark, by a gas pump, plays a pin-ball machine. He acts like a cartoon, popping his eyes and grimacing: "What's da mattuh, sistuh?"

Behind them, a dayglow pop art garage: bright-painted oildrums and rubber tubing. "Where did you get the address?"

Paula explains, "I remembered he was fond of cars, and I saw his Alfa."

"I told Donald to set fire to it," Widmark complains.

Paula lights a cigarette: "Why did you kill him?"

"What makes you think that?"

"You can tell that to a cinema audience, but it won't wash with me."

Widmark stands before the bright pinball playing board, all

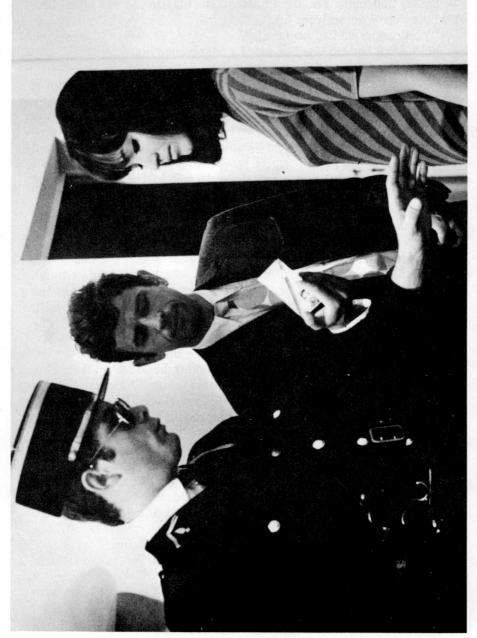

Paula (Anna Karina) encounters Widmark (Laszlo Szabo) and police state tactics.

bathing beauties and comets of color: "Why do you want to revenge Po — " (jet roar).

"For the sake of idealism."

"Ah, yes. I remember he said fascism was the dollar of morality."

The two talk disjointedly, facing the camera with a pop art background. Widmark: "He had some evidence as to who killed the mayor, so we had to suppress the evidence, and him with it."

Paula, flatly: "A second murder, in fact."

"Oh, yes. Here it was worse than Chicago or Marseilles."

A comicstrip frame: A man with a pistol defending a girl from some unseen enemy. Widmark: "You see, I'm the chief organizer for the whole of the fifth region."

A comicstrip frame: two question marks floating in balloons.

In a formal pose, like a double ID picture, Paula sits, Widmark stands. He speaks: "She learned that Po— was dead, and thought that when she arrived everything would be easy."

Paula: "I tell him it's all Chinese to me." She pulls up the corners of her eyelids, Chinese style.

Paula wanders about, pulls a tape from Widmark's pocket.

The scholarly-type makes another garden phone call as a jet flies over . . .

Closeup: The dictaphone operating, and Richard Po—'s voice, terribly loud, grating, harsh: "The idea of a permanent revolution is only valid if the diversity and the determination of the teams of political economists allow them to overcome the uncertainties of the conjuncture . . . "

It rumbles on, grating, abstract, vaguely revolutionary, hard to understand, painfully harsh: "The Independence of the colonies having put a provisional end to a fatalistic evolution of the regime, the conquest of the interior and the struggle for the presidency must open up new areas of activity . . . "

Paula walks back and forth. "You know, I could kill you right now." He speaks to the camera: "Here I am in my black suit and my colored tie and I tell her that I still have quite a few friends in Paris, and that one day they will be back in power again."

Paula: "All right, okay."

Donald appears, following Widmark around as he tosses her the raincoat and leads her out. Donald tries to act "tough," then plays with his puzzle. Widmark shoves him along.

In another building, over Richard Po's voice, Widmark leads them up a staircase, shows a pass to a cop, who admits them to Paula's hotel room, now full of detectives taking notes.

"To be filed. To demand that a nation's ideology should be founded not on an analysis of the divergencies of public opinion nor on the examination of solidly founded facts, but on what certain

**97**

bureaucrats might choose to divulge of the contents of secret archives . . . such procedures as these, comrades, are typical of a police state."

Widmark whispers to a detective, Aldrich, the man in the car. Doris Misoguchi in the Beethoven t-shirt is slumped in the shower. Blood runs from her nose. She is dead. On the bed, Typhus is swimming in pools of blood. A detective puts a mirror to his mouth.

Aldrich is seen alone, babyfaced in light suit and dark glasses.

Godard, voiceover: "Looking at the pair of them, I finally understood exactly what is meant by the adjective parallel applied to the police. The inspector looked like a former pupil of the sciences polytechniques. He shouted at me to be careful of these area management fellows."

The police experts walk past Paula. Closeups of Typhus on the bed, Doris in the shower. Aldrich catches Paula trying to conceal the revolver in the cookbook, has her handcuffed and taken away. At the door, Widmark shows a pass, and takes Paula with him.

In a courtyard, surrounded by green leaves, Paula sits on the staircase with Widmark, about them an air of complicity, even sympathy.

"Dick had no secrets. He was a liar: I knew him."

"Someone killed Typhus," Widmark argues. "Someone is searching for the same thing we are."

"I'm sure it was you who killed Dick. Why? I don't know yet."

"Oh, yes," Widmark tells her. "You'll see it hang together very well. You're getting on my nerves."

"So it was you then."

"Not exactly . . . let us say that there were several of us."

"And supposing I say what I know and what I've guessed."

"No, you won't do that. He thinks you're the one who killed Typhus. I'm the only one who knows that I was with you at the time."

Two of Aldrich's men come down and seize Paula as a jet booms over.

Widmark: "I'm coming, I'm coming, leave her alone."

Widmark leads Paula to Aldrich, sitting in a cafe before a huge blowup of an engraving of waves. Widmark tries to speak, is waved off. "That'll do." Aldrich unlocks Paula's handcuffs, brushes Widmark off again.

Paula, fullface: "I can't tell you how much I hate the police."

David Goodis' voice: "It's her." Paula repeats her remarks.

In closeup, a hysterical handcuffed Goodis: "Yes, she's the one who killed Uncle Edgar."

A young girl reporter joins the fray: "It's for *Atlantic City Magazine*. This Typhus, wasn't he Joe Attila's right hand man?"

"No comment." Aldrich hides behind his newspaper. Paula has no comment either.

In the garden, the scholarly assistant makes another phone call.

In the cafe, one of Aldrich's men reports. He reacts at once: "25 Rue Ben Hecht . . . I'll join you in the Peugot. A secret? If Richard Po— didn't die naturally, then he only could have committed suicide."

Paula is dubious. "With a bullet in the head fired from ten feet behind?"

"It's not the first time I've seen such a thing . . . "

In the courtyard, Paula sees Goodis handcuffed at the feet of two detectives. She leans down, turns his face to her, leaves.

Cut: Machinegun fire, blood splattered on a white background.

Cut: A young girl in green stands before a sink, a poodle in it. In a subdued voice she answers Paula, who remains offscreen.

"Was it she who telephoned me?"

"Yes."

"Why?" A jet roars over. "I told her not to be afraid."

"Well, I had tried to commit suicide."

"Was it that Richard told you something and they tortured you to find out what it was?"

"With a razor blade."

"What did he tell you? Are you afraid they'll start again if you talk to me?"

"Er, yes, yes."

Cut: The word *liberte*, painted in blue on a white wall, is shot up with a machine gun so the plaster flies off in lumps.

Cut: Paula stands before vivid yellow doubledoors with a red sign: *Sortie de Camions*. She wipes her eyes, walks off, enters a yard holding a huge pistol-wielding cowgirl, a movie house promotion. She meets the workman: "Excuse me, I'm the sister of Richard Po— (a bell rings). He worked here. He didn't leave a parcel or message for me?"

The workman doesn't know a thing.

In the workshop, two men pass with a huge panel of a cowboy shooting. The workshop is full of them: a Nazi on his head, a huge red face. A white-coated woman limps up past cutouts of two lovers, a girl in a swim suit, vulgar lettering, a Disney-style couple and a bear.

The woman: "Just now you mentioned Richard Po— (jet). He was kind to me. Once he asked me to do some accounts in a villa outside Atlantic City . . . Rue Preminger, something like that."

"Thank you," says Paula . . .

A cowboy cut-out passes, apparently self-propelled. Then a real man with a real tommy gun walks out. Paula comes to a car parked before a Walt Disney family. Widmark, out the window: "You've discovered something?"

"No more than you. Otherwise you would either leave me alone or have me disposed of. I think Aldrich is intelligent; he's told you what he thinks."

"What the hell does that matter! I'm the one in charge of the Fifth Region." (music begins) "What did you say to Goodis?"

"Nothing."

Widmark looks intent: "The person who killed Typhus is obviously the same one who knocked you out. It proves he didn't find out anything."

"And Dr. Ludwig?" Paula jabs. "Maybe it was him?" Widmark laughs. "Why shouldn't he be in the know?"

"Yeah . . . like you he's a valuable hostage, for me."

Paula gets in followed by the two detectives and the tommy gun man. They drive off as two men pass with a display panel of two sexy females: *Sexy Mondial*.

Godard, voiceover: "The deputy who lent him the Citroen had taken it back for the weekend, and Widmark returned me to the hotel in the killers' Chrysler, forbidding me to leave on pain of death, since I refused to tell where the villa was."

Cut: Paula packs her clothes on the bloodstained bed, Widmark waiting impatiently.

Cut: Paula crosses the screen as if trapped between Prussian blue steel walls. Beethoven chords. She comes back the opposite way.

Cut: David Goodis is typing with one finger in the hotel room. Paula waits for him restlessly, ruffles her hair.

Cut: On the bed, Paula uses the phone, David loads his silencer-pistol, gives it to her. She tries to fit it into the *Larousse Cookbook*, but it's too long now.

Jump cuts: She kisses him on the ear. Again, again.

Cut: Closeup of Paula against the window, face in shadow. Chamber music.

Cut: V.O., and more neon signs.

Cut: The tape recorder, with Richard Po—'s grating, blaring voice: "Yes, comrades, times have changed. But I tell you also that lies and deception are still with us, particularly among those who feel their social influence threatened. The present government is seeking to divert social pressure into patriotic propaganda and the glorification of nuclear adventure."

Cut: Closeup of revolvers in a shopwindow. Paula breaks the glass, seizes the smallest.

Cut: A grotesquely bandaged female figure, head and hands swathed in bandages with blood seeping through, stands by a blood-stained door. Music.

**100**

Cut: Paula, utterly bewildered, against a wall dappled with fragments of posters.

Godard's voice: "Then, first of all, as I was still a police suspect and Widmark was holding me, I telephoned him again and gave him the name of a man we both thought might well have killed Typhus."

The voice of Richard Po—: "A taste for conspicuous display which the Right is so fond of today and which affords to the multitudes the facile emotions of courage without danger and pride without sacrifice."

Closeup of Paula, listening in a dark room. She gasps: "Politics — money — it makes me sick to death to be involved in all this. Oh, Richard!"

Two black-and-white photographs, silhouettes of men fighting against a brick wall, and a heavy thug about to shoot a man about to shoot another man whose head he holds as an accomplice waits with the elevator.

Paula, in the garage: "It's just as I thought."

In silence, Donald walks away from her past the pinball machine, hits the machine, gesturing with his arms. Paula moves away, ducks under the hoist. Donald explains more and more frantically, his arms spread.

Godard's voice: "In order to revenge himself on his boss, Donald brought me photographs of Richard's death. We were certainly in a film about politics: Walt Disney plus blood" (two loud gunshots!). "He also told me it was he who childishly killed Typhus and his niece after they caught him searching my room. He confirmed that there was a villa, and offered to take me there for one million old francs, with which he was going to make off to South America. There, an idealist in his own way, he" (two gunshots!) "was going to finance an army of mercenaries to wipe out the Jews, the Negroes, the Chinese, and the Indians."

Paula: "If you had to die, would you prefer to know beforehand, or would you rather it was sudden?"

Donald would rather it was sudden. She shoots. He falls, dies clumsily on the floor, moaning: "Mamma . . . mama . . . mama . . . mama . . . "

Outside, Widmark waits, surrounded by gasoline and movie ads.

Richard Po—'s voice blares: "This is probably what some of those engaged in anti-Communist activity are afraid of."

In the garage, Paula searches Donald's corpse, finds documents.

Cut: Neon signs at night.

Marianne Faithful sings:
> It is the evening of the day
> I sit and watch the children play
> Smiling faces I can see
> But not for me.

Godard's voice: "To find out why Richard died was to find a reason for my continued existence."

Paula and David Goodis walk a narrow alley in bright sunshine, David making notes for his novel: "The memory of the chestnut curls comes back to him."

"Get out," Paula tells him. "It's the police . . . both our strange destinies . . . I'll see you in an hour at the villa, but now get out." She pushes David away as Aldrich arrives.

The inspector tells her: "You can leave Atlantic City if you like . . . I'm not interested in Typhus anymore . . . I've just received the order from Paris to close the whole affair provisionally. You shouldn't be surprised . . . it was you who invented that business of the false suspect." (He looks at a notebook.) "Dickson, Mark Dickson."

Paula asks if he's arrested him.

"I don't think it will be possible. He's already died in a fire . . . if we don't find him, he'll be condemned by default . . . Officially, only me and one other know he's dead."

"Monsieur Widmark?"

In closeup, Paula stands in a yellow dress among flowers. Aldrich: "Not Widmark. A young woman with a pretty dress — in fact, exactly like yours . . . "

They walk through the garden. Aldrich: "You're probably up to your neck in some political affair, which involves personal feelings — revenge, jealousy, friendship. If I were you, I would go back to Paris. There's going to be a nasty scene here . . . I'm telling you for your own sake."

Paula turns to him: "You know, we are in a part of the universe which is already old. Nothing much happens here, elsewhere whole galaxies are still exploding into life . . . "

Cut: Dr. Ludwig's scholar-assistant in a car reading a *Serie Noire* crime book, *Goodbye Life, Goodbye Love*. The camera pans to show Widmark in back. The two argue, for the assistant won't help him. Finally, Widmark says: "Tell Ludwig I'll call him this evening . . . "

Aldrich drives off, Paula hiding in an alley. She talks to his two assistants: "What's your name?"

"Robert McNamara."

"Aren't you fed up with all these assassinations?"

"It's my job. I enjoy it."

"I'm Richard Nixon. I'm in the same business."

"Right," she concludes. "As long as you're keeping me under observation, let's go see your boss."

They take her to Widmark in his car. One tries to take pictures, but the head of the Fifth Region shoos him away: "Get lost."

Cut: The word *liberte*, red on a white wall, is shot up by machine gun.

Cut: Paula against a wall, facing the camera: "I have still got my red and yellow dress on, but my voice has changed. I tell him its disgusting to have tortured that woman to get the address of the villa.

Cut: Widmark faces the camera before a similar wall: "It's not the first time I've had blood on my hands." (he raises them)

Cut: Paula looks to Widmark. "It's always the same — blood, fear, politics, money. I don't know how to stop vomiting since I've been working in all this. Oh, Richard — "

Cut: Closeup of paperback cover: *Cache Annee Zero (The Lowest Point of the Left)*.

Paula and Widmark, side by side before a green poster. They speak simultaneously to the camera:

Paula: "He tells me it was Richard who assassinated Paul La Croix, they started a fire. At the time, the party wanted to pin everything on their Socialist allies. In this region that suited them fine. The reason why Richard met the same fate in the end is that his methods were a little too personal. At least, that's what I believe. Me, I shall never get out of it now." (machinegun fire!) "I would have done better not to listen to that little Donald and gone back to Paris. Now I'll have to play it out to the end. I'll have to act, make believe, instead of lying on a beach in Italy, and dreaming in the water and the sun . . . once . . . "

Widmark: "I took the precautions of sending the others away. If I'm going to get rid of Paula I don't want any witnesses. I told her it's a villa where the party used to have clandestine meetings unknown even to its own militants two and a half years ago, in '67. They decided to sabotage the alliance with the Federation of the left and blame everything on them. That's how it all started: La Croix, the former mayor, Richard Po— . . . the friends of Mendes France. They had to be shut up. And now, because of that, we still have to struggle and intrigue, assassinate, eliminate the adversary, instead of exercising power in peace, opening dams, keeping the currency healthy . . . one day . . . "

In a well-kept, spacious garden of an ultra-modern villa, abstract sculptures stand in bright sunshine. Paula walks the garden path before Widmark. Paula sees Goodis in the bushes, motions him to a better hiding place. Widmark leans against the glass wall, Paula wanders . . .

"You're quite right," she says. "Neither of us has any confidence in the other, there are too many things at stake."

Widmark: "Perhaps you're right. We must be able to trust each other."

Goodis runs to a better hiding place.

"There's just one way," Paula tells him. "I could give you a weapon which would turn against me if I betrayed you — a letter that it was I who killed Edgar Typhus."

"Yes, that would work."

"But you would have to write a letter too . . . saying that you killed Richard Po— " (sound of jet).

Godard's voice: "Yes, the question was how to keep alive, because otherwise, sooner or later, I would end up like the seventeen witnesses to Kennedy's death, who according to *Le Monde* of October tenth were all assassinated too."

Widmark tears the finished letter out and gives it to Paula. They read the exchanged confessions:

Paula: "It was I who killed Richard Po— " (a jet blots out the sound). "He was trying to extort money from me. And his death was an accident. Dr. Ludwig knows all about it. He helped me to hush up the affairs thanks to his numerous political contacts.
Richard Widmark, 17 September 1968.
Is that right?"

Widmark: "It was I who killed Edgar Typhus. He came to my room. We had an argument. I knocked him out with the ashtray.
17 September 1968
Paula Nelson."

Paula takes a few steps from Widmark, his note in her pocket.

Widmark comes into the frame pointing a revolver at her. He takes her gun, unloads it, returns it, takes back his letter. Widmark: "Don't move, you've found out, otherwise you wouldn't have had the idea."

"But I haven't found out anything. There's no secret, no . . . "

He makes her come back to the glass wall, his back to it. Behind him is David Goodis, who kills Widmark.

Paula: "Yes . . . thank you, David."

Goodis puts away the gun, brings out the little notebook of his novel, and writes, taking his inspiration from Widmark's corpse. Paula strokes his hair.

*Far from time and space, men have lost their way*
*Thin as a hair, broad as the dawn, their ears foaming,*
*Their eyes turned up, hands outstretched, groping for the*
*decor, already not there. Thank you, madame —*
*Now I shall be able to finish my novel."*

But Paula objects: "No David. You must prepare yourself for death . . . if you finish your novel, everyone will know it, for beauty is truth."

"But why, madam, always talk in metaphors?"

Paula loads her revolver, chanting:

"If I speak to you of time, it is because it has not come
If I speak to you of a place, it is because it is no more
If I speak to you of a time, it is becaust it has gone before
If I speak to you of a man, it is because he'll soon be done."

She shoots Goodis in the forehead.

"Oh, Paula, you have robbed me of my youth!"

Closeup of Paula, crying: "Oh, David . . . sadness."

Closeup of dictaphone, spools rotating, Paula's voice flawlessly: "Where am I? Is it me who is speaking? Can I say that I am these words I speak, through which my thoughts slide? Can I say that I am these murders I have committed with my own hands, actions which escape from me not only when I have finished, but before I have even started. Can I say that I am this life which I feel within me? It envelopes me all at once with irresistible time . . . "

Closeup: Paula in a dark room, listening to the dictaphone.

"The night is long as the day in this enternal equinox. Night is falling, I go on . . . I will leave once more before the dawn . . . "

Closeup of dictaphone, of Paula, of dictaphone.

"Birth, death, the duration of the things which surround me and the duration of my own body, my body which embraced Richard, my knowledge of these things is necessarily and by its nature incomplete and deceptive, as I can know them only through the modification of my body and my thoughts."

Paula waits at a traffic light, her hair bllowing. Red . . . green . . . red.

"The drama of my consciousness is that having lost the world, I try to recover myself, and in this very movement I am lost . . . " (she recognizes a car) "Phillipe!" (music)

A yellow EUROPE No. 1 commercial radio car, driven by the journalist Phillipe, drives up. He sees Paula, pulls over — what's he doing here?

"Oh, me I've been doing a bit of reporting for *Europe*."

"I've just been mixed up in a shady affair . . . I killed two people. Can you take me away?"

Closeup of *The Lowest Point of the Left* paperback. Schuman's Fourth Symphony surges forth.

They drive steadily through a very sunny day.

"There's no need to be afraid," Phillipe tells her. "Fascism will never succeed."

"It will succeed inevitably," — "and it will pass, like sailing, mini-skirts, rock and roll. But there are still many years of struggle, and often they will be internal struggle. That's why I'm afraid — of being tired before hand, of giving up the fight."

She takes a cigarette, plays with it.

"You know, as far as Richard is concerned, it was more an act of revenge, but your story isn't very clear."

"And the Ben Barka affair, was that clear? But I still have my principles."

"Are you still working at *Radar*? . . . Are you going to write an article, perhaps a book, like the one you were going to do on Oswald?"

"Oh, yes."

"In that case, you can't say you have any principles, Paula . . . they'll never change, no, no!"

"What?"

"You remember Elizabeth in **Les Enfants Terribles?**" He raises his finger. "The Right and the Left, they'll never change. The Right because it's stupid as it is vicious. The Left because it's sentimenatl. Beside, the idea of Right and Left is an equation which is totally out of date, one can't put it like that."

She faces the camera: "Well, how?"

She puts her hand up, turns, straightens her hair, can't sit still.

END appears in the frame, E in red, N in white, D in blue, as in French or American flags.

There have been several interesting critical approaches to **Made in U.S.A.**, all derivable from the title. McBean (5.10) sees much of the film as an American painter's cinema, "told in color, composition, and light." Godard clearly uses the violent splashes of color of the "action painters" but transcends even their violence, painting often in blood — the bed where Typhus dies is the clearest example, composed shots of it resemble a Jackson Pollack painting.

Godard also borrows techniques from the American comic strip. As well as the insertion of actual comic strip frames, he uses frame-to-frame cutting on lines, as well as holding a shot on a pondering character — as if waiting for a thought balloon to form. There is also plenty of Dick-Tracy-type gore.

Pop Art antecedents are plain in the brightly painted garage interior, the dayglow traffic signs, the machinegunning of **liberte** in assorted delicious colors. Pop Art and the comic strips overlap in the Beethoven sweatshirt and the direct, abbreviated narrative.

Raymond Coutard's compensated wideangle cinematography produces a series of always beautiful, illuminated shots, what one critic calls "widescreen postcards from an infernal Disneyland." This excellent camerawork has a high-budget American production gloss to it, although it was accomplished with Godard's fast-and-cheap production technique. McBean recalls that Godard admired Agnes Varda's **Le Bonheur** and wanted to mimic aspects of her style, to have the viewer get "inside the image." Karina's first words are in fact "Le bonheur" (happiness), and the actress is seemingly offered up to the audience's caresses, on the screen nearly every minute and frequently in closeup, posed against brightly colored walls, like a series of paintings: Karina on Blue, Karina on Red, Karina on Yellow, often endearingly (or annoying) fluffing out her soft dark hair. McBean is likewise aware that with this beautiful, poker-faced femme fatale Godard is mocking the aggressive, sexually exploitative American production conventions. This one aspect of a major theme of **Made in U.S.A.** – an examination of Europe's "American mutations."

Several critics, notably Raymond Federman (5.6), consider the "American mutations" of Europe and Europeans a major theme in all Godard's work. These are scattered all though **Made in U.S.A.**: obvious ones include a French "Atlantic City," tommy guns, Chryslers, pinball machines, and numerous American folkways. Societally, Americanization in **Made in U.S.A.** is shown at the cultural level in civilization and art, at the social level in institutions and relationships, and at the political level in intrigue and violence.

Culturally, French civilization and art is mocked by the American presence, from Chryslers and Hollywood characters to gangsterism and a police state. The artist David Goodis (Godard's joke, the real Goodis wrote *Down There*, the source of **Shoot the Piano Player**), is irrelevant to everyone and casually eliminated as a possible threat. People read only magazines, political tracts, and detective stories.

Socially, **Made In U.S.A.** is a copy of a copy, the assassination of President John F. Kennedy, and the seventeen coverup killings that followed a model for the plot, even alluded to in the script. The eighteen deaths are a model for this society, "a thin crust of coherence over violence and intrigue" (5.8), a police state divided up into regions for effective supervision, with overlapping "parallel police." Human relations here (Paula-Richard, David-Doris) are a fragile liabilities, quickly destroyed. Betrayal, distrust, treachery are the norms. Hired killers are named Robert McNamara and Richard Nixon.

Politically, **Made in U.S.A.** displays the worst aspects of American "crypto-fascism" government, police and politics sinisterly linked: Widmark's tri-color pass giving him police immunity; orders from Paris closing down the investigation; Richard's girlfriend tortured with a razor blade. Political power is shown to come from the barrel of a gun: Ian Cameron (5.2) notes that the plot is simply units of pure violence, the issues are corrupted by Typhus' and Donald's greed and Paula's lust for revenge. Liberty itself is riddled with machine gun bullets. At the end, Godard and Paula are back where they started.

These societal asides are part of a complex attitude of Godard's towards America's influence on life. Godard's feeling is obviously not all negative – he is enthusiastic about action painting, comic strips, and American films of the thirties and forties. (He salutes them with Rue Ben Hecht and Rue Otto Preminger.) Yet for the most part Godard opposes the "American mutations" – Federman thinks he sees them as remaking life itself in imitation of the American system, thus ultimately "prostituting" everyone, making them live by and paying them off in fashions they would not really choose. Thus, the "Version Originale" of Donald is silly and whimsical, wearing an absurd button and playing with a toy, but not a vicious killer. Likewise, Paula, seemingly motivated by a Hollywood-type-thirst-for-vengeance is gradually corrupted by the labyrinth of plots and subplots, in the end totally confused, playing her own thoughts processes back on the tape to get some notion of what she has been driven to. McBean (5.10) sees Godard in a complex love-hate relationship with America, "fascinated yet fearful of our guns, gangs, gadgets, and Coca-cola."

It is in the film's ambiguities and confusions that some of the most interesting ideas lie. The narrative, deliberately confused and out of order, suggests to Roud (5.11) that Godard believed a coherent story would be false and dishonest, since even now we cannot understand aspects of the Kennedy assassination or the Ben Barka Affair. In the end, indeed, Paula is sure of little more than she was at the start.

McBean believes that a major theme of **Made in U.S.A.** is the idea of a situation or problem containing many signs and indications, all "partly" true, typified by the plot confusions, as well as such devices as the hiding of Richard Po–'s full name (King? Kennedy? Ben Barka? most appropriately, X?), the overlapping monologues, and the garbled tape which hints at revelations but in the end typifies Leftist incoherence. The philosophical discourses in the bar, among other things, show the ease with which language can lie and invert even obvious truths, beautifully counterpointed by the lovely full color images of Coutard's cinematography, made hypnotic by Karina's smooth pacing. McBean sees this theme of "sign overload" as reflecting the McLuhanesque dilemma of living in a society full of mutually contradictory options and directives, a difficulty also discussed in Toffler's *Future Shock*.

Part of the multiplicity of clues and alternatives in **Made in U.S.A.** is an implied running wild of the imagination, the signs and symbols taking on terrible latent power and meaning. In the work-shop, surrounded by the cut-out screen personalities, Paula seems to be caught inside the "Hollywood hallucination," a cowboy figure moseying out the door, a gangster with a tommy gun striding out into the real street. The myths are "taking over" in the most straight-forward fashion, producing a huge horror comic come to life, as an all-American Disney family, rifles in hand, look on with steadfast approval. Likewise, the agents and assassins in the bar are all sub-dued by Marianne Faithful's plaintive "It is the Evening of the Day," the words taking on ominous force. McBean suggests the title line hints at the very decline of the West, while "children doing things I used to do" implies the New Europe's repeating American mistakes, and sitting and watching through bitter tears indicates our collective impotence. Both these sequences contain a self-mocking element, Godard aware of his teasing, yet "stamping the world 'Made in U.S.A.' – violent, stupid, sterile, based on imitating illustions." (5.6)

Of course, not all of Godard's playfulness can be taken as com-mentary. When David Goodis speaks of seeing his girlfriend every single moment for 127 years, Godard is mocking a romantic in love. Likewise naming peripheral characters Mark Dickson, Ruby Gentry, and Daisy Canyon, Godard seems to be using a quick, sardonic short-hand to "establish characters" rather than to be telling us his world is like a bunch of bad old movies, as one critic suggests.

The character of Paula Nelson seems to be at the center of much of **Made in U.S.A.** Ian Cameron suggests that she incorporates Godard's conclusions about the political establishment, being Left Wing in her dedication, Right Wing in her pattern of action. Like both sides nowadays, she feels a little well-placed violence will sort things out, but has little to show for it but a trail of corpses. Prog-nosis: total schizophrenia.

Paula goes through three stages politically. Initially, she is ap-palled by death and violence, though her feelings for Richard Po—lead her to make inquiries after him. It is in the bar, a philosophical limbo, that she sees the investigation as fundamentally orienting her, its morality setting up a zero point for her world. McBean (5.10) feels the French is more exactly translated as ethics, the implication of her monologue that a "person" is nothingness, creating himself every moment by the act of choosing. One is what one does, an abstract restatement of Godard's "the very definition of the human condition should be in the *mise en scene* itself." (5.10) McBean sees this credo as Godard's solution to the multitude of signs – Paula neither submits nor retreats, but remains assertive and self aware. In Kustow's phrase (5.9), she assumes her responsibilities.

Yet Paula's second attitude is still insufficient for the labyrinth of intrigue and treachery she has entered. In the end, her assertion turns to self-doubt, and she acknowledges the limitations which have led her into a strange complicity. Kustow (5.9) notes her discovery on the tape that one who even tries to speak some truth is tainted by its implied opposite, like the hidden, inverted meanings of the simple statements in the bar. For "truth's sake," Paula winds up killing the harmless David Goodis. The secret truths of politics, like the recorded secrets to Richard Po—, seem just grating, garbled, only painful meaninglessness. (Paula's message, recorded by the same mechanical means, is perfectly clear in quality.)

Godard's comments on **Made in U.S.A.** that the shot with the phrase *Gache, Annee Zero* (The Lowest Point of the Left), shown with the beginning of a movement of Schuman's Fourth Symphony, "represents a moment of hope. You can call it false, ridiculous, childish, provocative, but it is what it is, like a scientific object." (5.4)

The last few moments of **Made in U.S.A.** suggest some sort of optimistic vista: an open horizon, soft natural morning light, direction and purpose and easy speed, pleasant intelligent companionship, all to the flowing lines of Schumann. Paula seems to be herself again; coy, canny, self-possessed, ultimately hopeful while ready for struggle. Suggestively, the vehicle she travels in is EUROPE No. 1, and there is no taint of America, except for Phillipe's remark that her infatuation with Oswald or the incident just past shows her lack of principles. Phillipe sums up her previous character with the limitations of Right and Left, bringing the film to where it started. In reply, Karina faces straight into the future: "Well, now?"

# John Schlesinger

# MIDNIGHT COWBOY

John Schlesinger's previous films include **Billy Liar** (1963) and **Darling** (1965), like **Midnight Cowboy** about naive, young people struggling with the complex, demanding and sometimes cruel social environment, and their own self-destructive drives. **Billy Liar** concerns a sweet, dreamy, irresponsible adolescent clerk whose tendency to retreat into fantasies of freedom and power cause a great deal of various sorts of pain to his stifling but gruffly decent lower class family and friends, some of it amusing. In the end, he lets slip a romantic chance to escape with a beautiful, free-living girl, into a life that might engage him, and it's implied that he prefers his fantasy, and fumbling.

**Darling** chronicles the life of a bitchy young model in "sophisticated" London society, from affairs to abortion to two-timing an earnest lover, to a marriage into Italian royalty that amounts to personal exile. The film includes satirical hints at corruption and perversion among the semi-artistic set, brilliant executives, and political figures. The girl tells her own story but, like Billy Liar, doesn't seem aware of her motives; she just cheats or swings or plays house because the chance is there — it will give some kind of kick, and can be covered up on a way to a "groovier scene." (Her responses are if anything less coherent.) In the end, she chooses exile with the foreign prince 20 years her senior, perhaps as a way to keep her impulsiveness, which she has come to fear, in check.

In interviews, Schlesinger has implied similarities between **Midnight Cowboy** and his previous films. He feels that one theme runs through all: "The problem of finding security and happiness and the need for accepting second best when it is forced on one." (6.10) "Nothing is really accomplished without great effort . . . and Joe Buck arrived in New York without an idea of life. The odds were against him . . . **Midnight Cowboy** is not about the seamy side of life, it is about a commitment Joe Buck makes to Ratso. When Buck finally makes it as a hustler, what does he do? He tries to save Ratso! Instead of keeping a date . . . and making 20 bucks, he beats up a masochist for the bus fare, and takes Ratso to Florida." (6.11) Schlesinger's common themes include learning one's true nature and the nature of society, the satisfactions and joys of relating with others, and the forces which destroy such relationships.

There were little homosexual bits in **Darling**, but **Midnight Cowboy** is the first time sexual deviations have been a good part of Schlesinger's storyline. He comments that such scenes are common in American films now (e.g., **The Detective, The Sergeant, Reflections in a Golden Eye**). "It comes from what's happening all around. Everybody does more or less what he wants to these days, and no one asks anything about it. Films are reflections of that attitude, and homosexuality is just one part of the whole scene." (6.10) Schlesinger states the film shows how two men can have a meaningful relationship without being homosexual.

In commenting on his own work at this stage of his career, Schlesinger concluded: "Inevitably a director's own attitudes will creep subconsciously into his films. Any film that is seriously made will also reflect the attitudes of contemporary society. It is possible . . . to give entertainment that will nevertheless provoke thought, disturb the mind, and stir the imagination." (6.10)

Schlesinger can be characterized more as a social commentator and critic than an artist realizing a private vision (pace Antonioni) or a skilled craftsman turning out his own style of genre picture (Boorman, perhaps). This attitude towards moviemaking clearly has its own built-in problems when the filmmaker works abroad. Straightforward social commentary is harder to justify than artistic insights or dramatic points, since it must originate in the special qualities of the given society. **Midnight Cowboy** anticipates this problem in several ways. Schlesinger let native novelist James Leo Herlihy write his screenplay (6.7), which follows the original storyline and tone. Second, he worked with a pair of excellent American actors, often clearly giving them their head. Finally, he had a location (the forty-second street area) whose ambiance is complex but never in doubt, and apparently tried hard to catch its full flavor: "a mixture of violence, desperation, and humor." (6.10)

The screen is pure bright white.

Faintly, a child's yell: "Bang! Bang-bang-bang! Yippee!" The camera zooms back to show a little boy wildly rocking a hobby horse under the mammoth screen of a Texas drive-in. Around it we see the flat western immensity, silent and golden under bright blue.

A rush of water, a young twanging voice: "Git along, l'il doggies!" A fresh-faced youth showers, singing.

In a greasy kitchen, the fry cook scowls: "Where's that Joe Buck!"

In his room, a grinning Joe dons the best in Roy Rogers drag: a blue cowboy shirt embossed with peacocks, tan slacks, buckskin-fringed jacket with hand-tooled boots. Resplendent, he collects his dishwasher's pay, announces he's headed East: "Lotsa rich women back there, beggin' for it, payin' for it, cause the men is all tooty-fruities!"

Outside, he hesitates. But: "What the hell I got to hang around for? I got places to go!" He swings a black-and-white horsehide suitcase onto the Greyhound bus.

The NEW YORK bus cruises the sunlit turnpike. "Bang-Bang!" It's Joe's transistor radio, his constant companion: "It's the shooting season, folks!"

A young woman sits, he twangs a lively greeting. A shy girl-child peeks over the seat, his eyes light up. Joe dozes: the bright bus interior dissolves to dark fragmented images:

A lovely anxious girl pleads with a younger Joe: "Do you love me Joe? You're the only one!" A pack of hoody, excited youths stalk them, taunting, cruel: "You're the best Joe, the best!" The girl, Crazy Annie, cries as they thrash on a bed in an abandoned house: "Do you love me, Joe, do you love me?" Crazy Annie runs, terrified —

"The Jesus Saves Hour!" The radio brays: "A sister just sent ten dollars and two malignant tumors she coughed up!" The pike is lined with dismal stands and shacks, a sign mocks: "World's Largest Hotdogs!" at Joe. The spellbinder: "Jesus wants to know how many sent in five dollars for their home worship kits!" Joe cuddles the radio.

The Greyhound runs on, the yellow headlamps probing; a gray woman, the kid massaging her back, the two cuddling in bed . . .

The bus surges on. A sign atop another shack: JESUS SAVES. The transistor plays the film's theme, a cheery: "I'm goin' where the sun keeps shinin', through the pourin' rain!" Joe grins and snuggles up to the radio in his fancy cowboy suit. The bus races on . . .

Joe peers at the Statue of Liberty, hears the crisp glib voice of the city: "Seventy-seven, radio New York! This is Ron Lundy, this is WABC!" The station wants to know what women are looking for:

"I like Gary Cooper, but he's dead." (Joe puffs up his chest.)

"A man who takes pride in his appearance." (Joe grins, rolls his shoulders.)

"Someone I can talk to in bed!" (He smiles cruelly.)

"A rebel!" (Joe snorts in delight.)

"Young!" (Joe grins.)

"You!" (Joe gives a rebel yell of joy.)

To the Marine Hymn, the Greyhound soars over the Jersey flats towards the city skyline . . .

In a plain room above Times Square, the boyish Texan turns on his transistor. A woman wails: "My remedy for insomnia — "

"Just dial for Joe Buck!" he finishes.

Still in stetson, boots and fringed jacket, Joe prowls the city looking for the action: "You sure are a pretty lady . . . "

"You ought to be ashamed of yourself!"

Joe walks on. Under Tiffany's window, jewels blazing, is a man sprawled unconscious or dead. The crowds boil past, ignoring him. Joe stares, vaguely horrified . . .

Joe stares from his window at the MONY building. Below a poster of an icy-eyed Paul Newman, the TV shows a poodle in pants and coat. "They got you all gussied up!" Joe kids doubtfully. The TV prattles on . . .

On a bright Park Avenue island, Joe meets a flabby, dead-eyed dowager: "Where's the Statue of Liberty, ma'am?"

"It's up in Central Park taking a leak!"

But in moments she has him in her penthouse. Blonde, fiftyish with a hard, petulant face and a white poodle, she clutches the dog and coos over the phone to a sugar daddy while Joe kisses and caresses her from behind. She turns him to unbutton his shirt, lets him kick off his pants. Laughing, naked, they collapse into an immense bed.

In the frame are only their grappling legs, and beyond a TV screen: "Welcome to Dateline," it announces sardonically, "in our isolation booths — "

The channel changes, somebody's bouncing on the control. Screen: A man does pushups: "One-two, one-two, one-two, one-two!"

Change! A dragon belches flames! (Oh, wow!" the dowager moans.)

Change! A sober cardinal: "Is God dead?"

Change! Bette Davis emotes all over the screen.

Change! More pushups, endlessly. (Oh my God!" the dowager cries.)

Change! A child.

Change! A building collapses.

Change! A sober Cardinal.

Change! Bette Davis, weeping and wailing.

Quick changes: Man with a fat cigar! Woman's mouth gasps! Ultraman! Man with a fat cigar! A woman's mouth gasps! Ultraman! Man with a fat cigar! A woman's mouth gasps! Ultraman!

Change! A slot machine spins and roars.

Change! The push-up man grunting away.

Change! The slot machine hits — coins pour on jangling! . . .

The woman, Cass, stretches: "Knock off a few pounds and I'd

really be a gorgeous chick!" But now she won't let Joe see her, touch her. Joe stands in amazement: A real penthouse! Cass smiles. "You make me feel so damn at home, I almost hate to bring up business." Cass needs a few bucks.

The buckskinned ingenue, bewildered: "I was just about to ask *you* —

Wrathfully: "Me! In case you didn't notice, I'm one hell of a gorgeous chick!" She turns on him: "Will you get *out* of here!"

Joe backs away: "How much do you want? Five, ten, twenty, there you go!" She stuffs it into her bosom . . .

In a dim barroom, a short greasy-haired wise-eyed man turns to a thoughtful Joe Buck. "Terrific shirt," he rasps.

"You talking to me?"

A B-girl asks for a cigarette, and the runt grabs at the pack. "Oh, kiss it Ratso!" the girl whines.

"Joe Buck, from Texas," Joe grins.

"Enrico Rizzo, from the Bronx." The voice is thick, rasping.

Joe buys the drinks, opens up: "She busts out bawling when I ask her for money . . . How'm I supposed to know? You gotta tell a person these things."

Ratso looks him over: "You know what you need? O'Daniel. He operates the biggest stable in town. You know, a dame cries, I'd cut out my heart . . . "

The B-girl drifts past: "I'd call that a minor operation."

Ratso turns on her: "I'm used to these types that pick on cripples. The sewers are full of them."

Joe is suddenly aware of Ratso's bad leg.

They push through the crush, Ratso with a determined swinging limp, talking, talking: "The girls gotta have some kind of a middleman — O'Daniel . . . you should take in $50, $100 a day, easy — "

He gets ten dollars for the lead. Protesters parade past. "Get outa here, ya bunch of creeps," Ratso yells. "Go to work!"

Crossing a street a cab leaps at them, Ratso braces his arms on it, snarling, almost claims an injury.

O'Daniel, a pop-eyed balding fiftyish man welcomes Joe to his dreary rooms: dirty walls, piles of clothing, airshaft beyond the window. The old man pats him from behind: "Strong back. So you want to help, eh! cowboy."

Joe grins: "Well, I ain't a for-real cowboy . . . but I sure am one hell of a stud!"

O'Daniel grins, putting his hands on Joe's shoulders and staring at him. He bets Joe's lonesome: "Lonesome as a drunk, a dope fiend, a thief, a fornicator . . . "

Joe's face is a mixture of pleased acknowledgment and nervous

**115**

suspicion. "Why don't you and I get down on our knees right now?" O'Daniel grins. "I've prayed on the streets, in saloons, toilets, it don't matter where — long as He gets that prayer!" . . .

Bright shards of images: Little Joe baptized at the riverbank, splashing, choking, the congregation smiling . . .

"Don't run from Jesus!"

Joe slams through the apartment, twisting from O'Daniel's pop-eyed ecstatic face to a plastic electric Jesus mask which flashes at him! . . .

Joe runs across Times Square, blazing with neon.

He stumbles into the chattering subway, sees Ratso, chases. A burst of stark staccatto images:

Ratso on the phone, Joe grabs him, chokes —

The deserted subway station, grimy, glaring — Joe runs through it —

The wild pack chases young Joe. Crazy Annie screaming in headlight glare, her lovely face terrified in blue-white blaze. The wild pack pounds after — yelping —

Joe sees Ratso hop a local, runs for him, furious —

The wild pack attacks Crazy Annie and Joe, screaming, struggling — Ratso, strangled by Joe, slumps —

The bartender knows nothing. Joe raises the bottle to hurl . . . but sets it down . . .

Joe walks shabby, daytime Times Square, passing overpriced restaurants, drab pornography shops, movies, ugly rushing mobs. A rich radio voice murmurs: "Gold, silver, candlelight, wine, sky-rockets, butterflies — watch them glitter . . . "

A hotel clerk regards Joe distrustfully at the desk: "We'll keep them nice and safe until you get this thing settled." Joe goes out into the street, evicted, possessionless . . .

A window sign: DISHWASHER WANTED. Joe looks at it and murmurs: "You know what you got to do, cowboy."

Dark figures slumped, some dozing, in a shabby theatre. On the screen, two science fiction spaceships tersely orbit: "Spacecraft, we have a malfunction . . . "

A skinny college student, all acne and hornrims, paws and kisses Joe.

The spaceship crackles: " . . . we've lost contact . . . "

Shard of an image: Young Joe and a crazy Annie make love.

Shards of images: Joe held helpless on a carhood, the pack of youths assaulting Annie in the headlights. A mocking voice: "Kissing Crazy Annie? You'd better swallow the drugstore!" "Joe, love me more, Joe!"

In the moviehouse men's room: the boy vomits into a basin. Joe whispers fiercely for his money.

"I don't have any!"

Joe grabs his watch, but the kid pleads: "I can't go home without it, my mother would die!" Joe snarls: "I don't want your damn watch!"

The midnight cowboy wanders wearily at dawn, his radio piping. He blinks. It's Ratso, greasy and unshaven, in a doughnut bar: "C'mon, don't hit me, I'm a cripple!"

"Where's my money!"

Ratso pulls out all his cash. "It's sticky, what'd ya do, slobber on it?"

The two eye each other distrustfully, Joe in his cowboy suit, Ratso in a shapeless black coat: "I'm invitin' you," Ratso slurs, "I gotta place" . . .

They work their way into a dark empty hulk of a brick building, the windows whitewashed with Xs: "The X means the landlord can't collect the rent, on account of its condemned," Ratso mutters. "It keeps the punks and creeps out."

Joe lugs an old icebox upstairs ("It'll keep the roaches from getting into the perishables," Ratso explains). Home is a dilapidated abandoned apartment, with two bare beds, table and chair in an ancient kitchen. The walls are bare but for cut-out orange juice ads. The two shiver, curled on the beds. Ratso: "There's no heat, but by winter I'll be in Florida."

Joe sleeps.

Image shards: In a car, young Joe and Crazy Annie embrace joyfully: "Love me Joe!" A flash, it's Sally Buck. A flash, it's the wild pack. In flashlight glare, the two are wrestled out, the ratpack mauling Annie, beating Joe. The police siren up. A wrecking ball smashes at the apartment. Joe naked, hysterical, shoves at a wire fence while Annie wails away in an ambulance, crying out to him . . .

Joe shakes himself awake: "Where's my boots!"

Ratso took them off so he could sleep.

"What're you after, Ratso! You don't look like no fag . . . "

"Do me one favor," the grubby cripple rasps. "In my own place my name is Rico." He coughs.

Joe: "Rico, Rico."

In an outdoor vegetable market, Ratso and Joe approach a stand. "Stay 'way!" yells the owner. "Every time, you take stuff!" Ratso snatches a coconut . . .

At home, Ratso splits it, cooks: "The two basic items to sustain life," he lectures, "are sunshine and coconut milk. In Florida, you got a terrific amount of coconut trees . . . "

"Smells worse than it did cold," Joe whines.

"Miami Beach," Ratso muses. "Anybody could score there, even you . . . "

117

"When's the last time *you* scored?" Joe demands scornfully.

Ratso ignores it: "Frankly, you're beginning to smell . . . and for a stud in New York, that's a handicap."

"I bet you never even got laid!"

Ratso shrugs it off: "That cowboy crap is faggot stuff."

Joe doesn't pursue it, instead grins: "I like the way I look — makes me feel good, it does." With rising excitement: "and women like me, goddamn it! Only one thing I ever been any good for is loving — *I need management, God damn it!*"

Cut: Ratso cleans Joe's jacket at the laundromat, Joe shivering in a blanket. A sign reads: CREATIVE LAUNDRY.

Cut: Ratso kicks open a shoeshine box, waxes Joe's boots gleaming ("Hey, you're good!" "Faggot undertaker couldn't clean my old man's nails — buried him with gloves!").

Cut: Joe preens in a mirror, grinning.

Before an escort service, Ratso palms a dapper man's assignment, passes it to Joe: "I think we struck gold!" . . .

They stare upwards from the street. Ratso: "A whole hotel of lonely ladies. Score one, and with their talkin', I move an office in. *Get the cash!*"

Ratso watches him go . . .

In silence, Joe and Ratso in whites race along a bright beach, the cripple gradually outdistancing the muscular Texan . . .

Beside a hotel pool, Ratso gets a shine, Joe a manicure.

Ratso suavely calls out bingo numbers to a dozen gambling dowagers. Lovely bikinied girls call out to the refurbished hustler.

Suddenly, women in wheelchairs turn on Ratso in a skirmish line. He hurtles out over the pool . . .

In their shabby home, Ratso and Joe sit drinking coffee, blowing on their hands. The radio purrs: "It's going down tonight, folks, and we can expect snow flurries — " A commercial beats: "Orange juice, on ice, is nice! Orange juice is nice!" The two dance clumsily to it, trying to keep warm.

They stand in a pawnshop, the transistor on the counter: "I'll give you five."

In the apartment, a candle flutters in the gloom, Ratso coughs. They drag rags and newspapers over themselves to keep warm. Ratso rips off a piece, reads it.

Below the glaring grindhouse marquees, muffled shapes crowd to and fro. A speedfreak, high on pep pills, dashes back and forth, faintly shrieking. Joe shambles into a storefront: BLOODBANK — DONORS PAID.

In the dark apartment, Joe flashes his wad: "There you go, nine dollars!"

Ratso coughs, scrambles for a smoke. "That's smart — buy

yourself some medicine before you die on my goddamn hands!"

As wreckers pound at the tenement dispiritedly, Joe and Ratso wander away . . .

Gray tombstone rows below a gray sky. Ratso and Joe wander through . . .

"I hate boneyards," Joe mutters.

"So split, he ain't your goddamn father!"

They stand before a plot, and Ratso casually swipes a wreath. The shabby cripple looks at nothing: "He was even dumber than you. He couldn't even write his own name — just a big lousy X — like our dump, condemned!" . . .

The two sit in a drab luncheonette, all metal chairs and formica tables. A woman jabbers on a phone.

"It doesn't matter what you believe," Ratso ruminates. "Sometimes your spirit goes up, sometimes other places, some believe you come back in another body."

"I just hope I don't come back as yours!" Joe cracks, ignorantly cruel.

"I do some thinkin' about that stuff . . . " Ratso wonders, " . . . and I . . . do some thinkin' about it, that's all . . . "

A bizarre couple approach them, a young man with a Polaroid, a thick woman with an intense yet blank stare under frizzled hair. He flashes them, the girl gives Joe a leaflet. "Hey looka here!" the Texas announces. "I've been chosen for some damn thing — an invitation to a party!"

"It's a couple of wakos advertising . . . " Ratso sneers dully. "What do a couple of fruity wakos want with you and me?"

Joe argues him into going: "I'll just tell them I don't go nowhere without my buddy here!"

"I warn't dressin' for no party!" . . .

Night. The flaring ads blaze over Times Square: cigarettes, cars, deodorants. Joe studies Ratso at a loft entrance, wipes his face: "You're sweatin' all over the damn place!"

"Do I look okay?" murmurs a dizzy-looking Ratso . . .

A loft party, full of bizarre, affected types somnambulating through smoke, talking lackadaisically, intensely, or just staring. Polaroids flash, films are body projected, light-shows flicker amid clouds of cigarette smoke. A student-type smokes a joint.

An old actress poses on a corkscrew staircase: "I love everything in the theater. I would like to die on the stage."

A man dressed all in furs murmurs mystically: "My hair is fur, its tendrils reaching out into space sometimes. I've watched it touch many stars . . . "

A dazed Ratso: "Wakos!" He stumbles through weird cliquey crowds, clouds of illuminated haze.

119

Cut: The Superstar Ultra Violet fondles a cowboy boot.

The hosts greet Ratso: "There's beer and stuff behind you. Anything you want!"

"Oh, Jesus!" Ratso yelps, plunging towards the buffet, filling his pockets with luncheon meat, eyes darting furtively.

"It's like heroin," a wraithlike young man whispers: "Death is like heroin."

An attractive chunky brunette with a direct stare shares a joint with Joe: "Thank you, ma'am!"

Ultra Violet enters, movies are projected on her naked back. Joe puffs, Ratso gobbles. Images: Statue of an infant, two guests kissing, an Indian girl in sari, flashing lights, Joe laughing in the silvery-bright slashes of a strobe, Ratso jamming his pockets with food.

The hostess catches him: "Why are you stealing food?"

"I was just noticing you're outta salami. I think you . . . "

Dreamily: "It's free, you don't have to steal it."

"If it's free, than I ain't stealin' . . . "

"What's the matter," she asks vaguely. "How did you get crip pled?"

"I slipped on a banana peel," Ratso lunges away, sprawls on a couch, a great sunflower dropped on his chest. Joe staggers up with a silly grin: "Gues who I am?"

"Who?"

"Me!"

Images: bodies jammed together; kissing; more bodies; more kissing.

Joe and the girl begin hand games, kissing: "Let's leave now," she husks. "Your place or mine?"

Ratso is glittereyed: "She's hooked!"

"Why, cowboy-whore?" the brunette purrs. "Did you know we were gonna make it?" Suddenly confused: "Who's he? Don't tell me you two are a couple!"

Joe laughs: "Well now, I'll tell you the truth, I ain't a for-real cowboy — but I am one hell of a stud!"

"A very expensive stud," Ratso smirks, "I happen to be his manager — "

The girl gets rid of Ratso, asks the stud's name: "Joe — fabulous! Joe could be anyone. I love it! Move over, Joe! Come here, Joe! Kiss me, Joe! That's a good idea — kiss me, Joe!"

Ratso frisks the piled-up coats, tumbles down the stairs. "Hey fella, you fell!" Joe hustles Shirley into a cab, zooms off: "Hey Ratso, Whoopee-ki-ki-yo, boy!"

In her bright-yellow bedroom, Joe stares unhappily while the brunette wraps herself in furs: "Well, it happens."

120

"That's the first goddamn time this thing ever quit on me! That's a fact."

Shirley laughs . . . Joe snarls: "You think I'm lyin'?"

"No. I just got this funny image: a policeman without his stick, a bugler without his horn, etc., etc. . . . maybe we ought to take a little nap, and see what heppens . . . "

"I ain't sleepy!"

The two try Scrabble. "Shee-it!" Joe exclaims.

"There's an E in MONEY," she tells him.

MONY is on the board. "That's how they spell it up there on that big building — what in hell starts with Y?"

"It can end in Y . . . like LAY . . . "

Joe looks up: "That's enough cheating — teasing me so I can't think!"

But LAY does end in Y. Is that Joe's problem?

"I'm gonna show you what — " he begins, then assaults her, caressing, kissing, struggling, she bites him, Joe tumbling her over, Scrabble blocks stuck quivering to his ass, Shirley's legs thrashing. Shirley scratching, grinning, mean . . .

Shirley babbles away on the phone: "I'm not exaggerating, listen, Marge, you should try it, it might be terrific for you."

Joe shrugs: "Well I guess I could be available . . . I sure hate to trouble you . . . "

"Sure . . . Twenty dollars, wasn't it? . . . "

In the dark shabby apartment, Ratso sits unshaven, sweaty, shivering, coughing. Joe swaggers in with packages: "Hey, boy, I got some of that stuff you like to swill — aspirin, mentholatum, all that crap!"

Joe pours out soup. "We ain't gonna have to steal no more. We're gonna be riding easy before long."

"How was she?"

"She went crazy, if you want to know," Joe grins. "Turned into a damned alley cat!"

Ratso peers at him: "Don't get sore. I don't think I can walk anymore . . . I'm scared . . . you know what they do . . . when they find you can't walk, oh, Christ!"

Joe wants to get a doctor, throws another coat on Ratso.

"Florida," the cripple shivers, shudders. "You get me to Florida . . . just get me on a bus. They ain't sendin' me to Bellevue. Dumb, you're really dumb, some cowboy!"

"Dammit, shut up! Just when things are goin' right for me, you gotta pull a dumb stunt like this!" . . .

Joe is jammed in a phonebooth: "A goddamn good friend of hers! . . . Well, hell, I can't wait that long."

In a tacky shooting gallery, a balding thin-faced man in steel frame glasses introduces himself to Joe: "I'm in for a paper manu-facturers' convention and to have a little fun, dammit . . . if you could have dinner with me — oh, I forgot, I'm expecting a phone call at my hotel . . . "

Up in the hotel room, the man quavers: "This is terrible . . . You meet someone then . . . I want to give you a present for helping me be good." His skinny hand holds a St. Christopher's Medal.

Joe tells him: "I gotta have money . . . more than $10, I gotta have $57. I got family, dammit!"

"You're wasting your time," the businessman bites coldly, stuff-ing his wallet in the nighttable.

"Get out of my way, please, sir," Joe pleads, then hits him so the older man falls back. Joe's frightened, determined. "Please sir!"

"No, I deserved that, I brought this on myself," the man whines. Joe hits him so his nose bleeds, picks up the lamp: "Are you gonna let go of that table, or do you want a busted skull?" Joe socks him, the old man's false teeth knock loose. He snatches the wallet, but the businessman has grabbed the phone.

Joe walks back towards him, rips the instrument from the wall, pauses, then jams the receiver into the man's mouth as he writhes and moans . . .

A Greyhound hisses through the Jersey Tunnel.

"Thirty-one hours," Ratso stumbles. "11:30 in the morning, we get there. Not, this morning, but the next . . . you didn't kill him, did you?"

"I don't want to talk about it . . . "

The MIAMI, FLORIDA Greyhound rushes south. Ratso looks awful: unshaven, dirty, sweaty, ratty hair, but now his eyes are vague, the mouth loose, the cunning gone slack. He shivers beside Joe in the dim back of the bus, while highway lights hover, drift, or zip past beyond the windows.

"I hope we're not gonna have a lot of trouble about my name . . . can't you just see this guy running around the beach, suntanned, swimming — then somebody yells — 'Hey, Ratso!' "

"Sounds like I knew you," Joe tells him.

"Rico all the time, okay? Okay." Ratso whimpers in his seat, Joe watching him . . .

"I wet my pants, the seat's all wet," Ratso whines dully, "My legs hurt, my butt, my chest, my face, that's not enough, I got to pee all over myself . . . "

"You just . . . took a little rest stop that wasn't on schedule," Joe kids. They both laugh hysterically.

Joe emerges from a clothing store in slacks and shirt, puts his cowboy gear in the trash, goes into a restaurant. The waitress takes his order: "Ever been here before?"

"No, ma'am. This is my first time."

She smiles: "Well, I hope you have a good time in Florida." . . .

Joe slips on Ratso's new shirt and pants, lifts back onto the seat, wipes the sweat. "Thanks, Joe."

"Shirts are comfortable, aren't they? Yours was the only one left with palm tree." Joe lights a cigarette. Ratso coughs on it. throws it away . . .

"When we get to Miami, I'm gonna get some kind of job," Joe muses. "There must be an easier way of makin' a living than that! Okay, Rico? Hey, Rico?"

Joe shakes his shoulder, but Ratso doesn't respond. Gradually Joe realizes that he's gone . . .

The bus driver snakes back to their seat, turns: "Okay, folks, nothing to worry about." To Joe, softly: "Is he kin to you?" Joe nods, closes his eyes. "Well, nothing we can do. We'll just drive on in."

"Okay, folks!" the driver calls out. The passengers stare at them. "Just a little illness. We'll be in Miami in a few minutes."

Joe puts his arm around Ratso, holds him up.

Through the bus window the two of them, heads up, ride on through the green and blue seaside morning. The cheerful theme comes up . . .

One can discuss **Midnight Cowboy** by starting at the characters and working outward: for Joe Buck and Ratso Rizzo and their growing concern for each other are the context of everything else. At their best, they are beautiful Dickensian characters always ready to spill out of their roles, unloved castoffs of some unspeakable social dislocation, always threatened by a final grinding away into nothing.

Joe Buck, the fresh-faced title character, is a very American matrix of vulnerability and violence, brutalized so he can respond in only limited ways. Even after his friendship with Ratso is well begun, Joe cruelly insults the cripple in the cafeteria, and hides his concern beneath wisecracks. Joe's homosexual encounter with the CCNY student and its flashback dramatizes the fear, confusion and guilt that is so linked to sex in our culture — if not in a single spectacular trauma, then in chronic guilt, forbidden fantasies, and "imperfect sexual adjustments." As Canby (6.1) points out, Joe is "not ruthless enough" for success in the American system.

Enrico "Ratso" Rizzo is a paradigm of urban ethos, American style, a master of Warshow's "queer dishonest skills" of city life. He is shrewd and knowing, but trapped in a ruined body and a special social illegitimacy — no marketable skills. His defensiveness about his sexuality, appearance and background, and his resignation at his father's grave, all hint that like Joe he's too sensitive to succeed in this City of Dreadful Night.

The orchestration between these two is complex and subtle. The canny cripple and the ingenuous "stud" together approximate one healthy bright human being, and linked, steadily improve "its" fortunes. Their emotional interaction can almost be orchestrated: Ratso has a straight man to perform for, teach and feed bitterness; Joe — a sidekick with inside dope, encouragement, and flow of new ideas; both — someone to care about who cares about them, who they can respect and feel some contempt for. There is also a reversal of roles, Ratso giving Joe a place to stay, food, and grooming, but Joe in the end getting the getaway money, nursing Ratso towards Florida, and buying him new clothes. Joe also seems to abandon his own dream for Ratso's. It is on this story structure that the wider interpretations and comments on **Midnight Cowboy** that follow are erected.

As a commentary on American society, **Midnight Cowboy** is an attack on our commercialized culture, with notes on sex and religion. The theme of false advertising illusions versus a corrupted reality is established in the first shots — a kid in a drive-in playing two-gun cowboy, ignoring the quiet and beauty of the immense real range. Years later, Joe rejects the real, stifling cowtown, his Roy Rogers clothes and sincerity transforming him into a freak. Instead of a six-gun, the weapon often called "the equalizer" because it nullified social and economic power, Joe has only a transistor radio spewing lies and illusion. As he rides towards New York City in comfort, he constantly sees along the turnpike signs of privation and want.

The body of the film takes place in America's commercial inferno, Forty-Second Street and Broadway, where two goodhearted but limited young men find themselves virtually totally rejected, victimized, and brutalized. All Ratso's canny knowledge and guile, working with Joe's ingenuousness and masculine beauty allow them only the barest sort of survival, constantly undercut by social and personal abuse and degradation.

Schlesinger like Antonioni makes constant use of billboards and signs, always enticing but giving nothing. They glare and flare like strings of firecrackers, recalling the line about Times Square: "What a stunning sight, for someone who couldn't read!" Schlesinger is always cutting from the 40-foot Raquel Welches and advertising models to the grubby crowds beneath. A hovering fifty-foot Ban Deodorant can discharges over them like a napalming gunship. Over all towers the great MONY skyscraper — which Joe instinctively believes spells MONEY. Along Forty-Second Street's bright length — **This Is Your Perversion, The Fellatio Story, Holiday for Sadists** — homely, real people plod wearily, while a drug addict capers hysterically, ignored, frenetic as the ads. In the endless graveyard, the tombstones seem simply more proof that life is meaningless, driven by greed and illusions, futile in the end. A billboard on the horizon: HAVE A STEAK TODAY. Is this all? Ratso grabs a wreath from another grave, and the ambience of the scene makes it not crime, almost a model for every life in the film. Critics who argue that Schlesinger's attack on urban degradation is old-fashioned don't seem to notice his systematic, almost mystic dimensions.

The electronic media are equally shown up. Joe's transistor is constantly adding a false glow or cheerful background music to the most hopeless scene and situations. Occasionally, it's a morale builder: in one scene Ratso and Joe dance to an orange juice commercial to keep warm, but its commentary (about women, for example) is all false, suggesting the ill-advisor of Joe's journey, and in the end the Texan sells the sometimes-friend to help Ratso. The television is worse: the absurd panel discussions about the immorality of "naked animals" (based on a real hoax), shows the absurdity of enlightened social reform in a society poisoned by the buck. Joe's Rabelaisian channel-changing sex session has been criticized as too coarse, but I find it successful on several levels: as a simple bawdy interpretation of sex without sentiment; as a sly evasion of censorship; as a comic depiction of the sex act — rhythmic and emotional; as a send up of TV — a mass of titillating but barely diverting images. Likewise, the skin movies and science fiction film are shown as inhuman, tedious fantasies, time-fillers with perversion in the pit.

The Andy-Warhol-type party is a final social comment on the brutalizing culture of commerce. The well-heeled party goers are shown little happier or saner than Ratso and Joe. Like the crowds in Times Square, they dull their senses with dope, alcohol, and cigarettes, and escape into fantasies of light and film. The hostess shows only the most stuporous awareness to Ratso, likewise the girl Shirley is excited because her liason will require no intimacy ("Joe could be anyone — I love it!").

Schlesinger's critique of the personal corruption due to commerce is very tied up with his treatment of sexuality. True, there are other aspects, like the sprawled figure on the sidewalk — ignored by everyone, and the hustling cabman's sideswipe of Ratso matched by the cripple's readiness to fake an injury for the insurance. But in our money society, most character flaws show most clearly below the waist. Cass, the flabby matron Joe beds early on, likes it and obviously doesn't need money, but getting paid for intercourse has become a reflex. Likewise, Ratso instinctively exploits Joe's sexual misinformation, getting back at his dumb good looks, as does the CCNY student. In no recent film has sex been handled this coldly, as just pure vulnerability to be used to get something for nothing (*"Get the cash!*" Ratso exhorts). Sex has been used as a weapon, or the basis of mania or madness, but it is almost always an active force capable of being mishandled, like great strength. In **Midnight Cowboy** it becomes *solely* a handicap, a hemophilia, a way to be played for a sucker. Joe is *always* used, even if he gets paid. His body consciousness and sexuality work against his relationship with Ratso, jokes about the cripple's looks and sex making things just that much harder. Farber's complaint (6.5) that the friendship lacks "natural" homosexual overtones must be dismissed — it's obvious that Joe doesn't think of Ratso as a sexual creature at all, and the little man is too inhibited, sick and desperate to think about it for himself (it's notable that neither dreams or speaks of any sexual future, except at the end where Joe swears off mixing sex and money).

As the film goes on, the parallel between personal corruption, sexual maladjustment, and money worship, is drawn stronger and stronger. At the start, Cass's orgasmic-build-and-release was likened to playing and winning on a slot machine, coins pouring out at the "jackpot." The girl Shirley is excited at the very impersonality of her liason with Joe, but is dismayed at this relationship with Ratso. ("Are you two a couple?) My abbreviated treatment emphasizes lines but it still is made clear that there is something eerie about the contrasting relationships. Shirley does get her sado-masochistic kicks with Joe, after a temporary setback.

Schlesinger's point is stressed in Joe's attack on the masochistic businessman. The pack of boys, Cass, the CCNY students, Shirley, all have used Joe. Now, in desperation, he uses sex to take advantage of the businessman, finally attacking him for trying to use him. Some critics object to this sudden cruelty from a sympathetic character, but it can also be seen as Joe's first deliberate passionate act, a breaking out of the "fair play" which always ends up making him a sucker in this money-dominated world. An irrational act may be cruel, but it may also be forgiveable, especially in a corrupt world.

The mugging also suggests Schlesinger's judgment on the society he has depicted: crippling and cruel to everyone, the money society is bad because it makes real trust and sex a chancy and dangerous thing. One must be constantly watchful, an enervating and brutalizing condition for all concerned. The next time it may be jolly Cass or cool Shirley who gets worked over — both of them operate to make it likely. Meanwhile, everybody is ground away by casual indifference and exploitation.

A minor theme in **Midnight Cowboy** is a satire and condemnation of religion, especially fundamentalist religion. Thus, Joe's grandmother leaves his movie money under a plastic Jesus paperweight, and he's baptized, a terrifying experience, in the same community where the wild sex gang operates. Fundamentalists bray on the airways and squat along the highway, but none offer anything that could be called spiritual solace. O'Daniel, the New York preacher, has apparently gone mad in his squalid retreat, perhaps from trying to keep faith in such a Godless environment. ("It don't matter where, long as He gets that prayer.") The businessman-pervert offers Joe a St. Christopher's medal as a "present." Ratso dies with no mention of the church or afterlife, and it's clear in the cemetery that neither can believe, though Ratso wonders idly about it.

Art History I: The lions as beautiful animals: Viva, outrageously blasé; James Rado, ingenuously handsome; Jerry Ragni, an uninhibited cuddly bear (page 131 of text).

Agnes Varda

# LIONS LOVE

Agnes Varda comments: "Wherever I go, I make a new movie."
In Hollywood, in 1968 while her husband Jacques Demy was making
**The Model Shop** ("It was reason enough to come"), she realized her
own subtle optimistic vision of America: **Lion's Love.** The original
title was "Lions, Love and Lies," shortened, lightened and ellipti-
cized to **Lion's Love.** For Varda a word pair — not a meaning — it
might refer to the love of lions, love on a leonine scale, or lions in
love.

Like Demy, Varda sees her American film as a very personal
statement: "It's a collage of what happened to me in Hollywood in
1968. I was in Hollywood when McClure's play opened. I was there
when Kennedy's assassination happened. I watched it all on TV.
There I met Viva. And the only movies I saw in Hollywood I liked
were Andy's [Warhol] movies. So it's a collage of what I saw, how I
felt, whom I met. A collage called America, Hollywood, '68." (7.4)

Varda also classifies **Lion's Love** as a "subjective documentary."
The woman director has made a film that is very much herself, that
shows intensely what she sees, a technique first used with the stunning orchestrated images of **L'Opera Mouffee.** She told Jonas Mekas:
"**Lion's Love** shows my position in Hollywood, it's me. I recreate
life. I took all the actors, Viva, Shirley, Jerry, Jim, and I recreated a
'cinema lie.' I said, 'I'll take you as you are, but you won't be exactly
yourselves, you'll be always just on the edge of the truth — that is,
you'll be playing something you *could be.'*" (7.4)

In many ways, **Lion's Love** is concerned with the multi-leveled
and ambiguous nature of acting. Varda was impressed by "The
Beard" as art, but even more because it was performed in Hollywood, the movie capital where the real Harlow lived, worked, and
died. It inspired her to make her American film about film stars,
living and dead, the great actors past whose presence is still felt, and
the very different new generation. The film begins on a stage full of
overacting (for film) characters, striving for success and recognition.
Then, the camera draws slowly back to show a larger and larger

"stage," on which actors are stylized people, the force of events pressing us all willy-nilly into roles and stagecraft.

Varda says Shirley Clarke stands for herself, an independent filmmaker in Hollywood who fails to make a deal, is unsuccessful on their terms. In one scene, Shirley Clarke is supposed to take sleeping pills, but cannot "act that act," so Varda simply takes her place, though this was not scripted. Varda notes that at such points acting "becomes too difficult, becomes psychoanalysis." She is also interested in the monologues "where the actors started with the zero point of acting, where they could do anything they want for the camera, and then Viva says: 'I'd like to be in a real movie,' which shows that even her acting wasn't real. And then she really went to point zero, even the monologue was too much, she said — 'I want to breathe,' and she breathed, for one minute." (7.4) Varda also wanted the Kennedy family in the film because of its special "Shakespearean" style of acting — Johnson would have been a caricature. "Hollywood acting is related to political acting, to the political 'scene' or 'stage' . . . to succeed in politics, you have to do acting." Finally, McClure's 'The Beard' is acted out twice again, so the second time, in the swimming pool, the characters are "acting the act of acting . . . a ghost of acting."

In an interview (7.6) Agnes Varda comments that the old title, "Lions, Love and Lies" signifies the film's three main themes:

Lions. Actors are like lions, in fact the great ones were called Lions back in the 18th Century. The three players I chose look like lions, with all their hair. Or should I say, their manes? What is it like to be an actor in Hollywood today? What is the new breed of stars like? Who are the stars of today? Are political figures the best actors nowadays? Are they the real stars of our times? Are they also lions?

Love. The three main characters love each other. I love love stories. How could these three actors be in love? What kind of love would it be?

Lies. Are actors liars or not? Are politicians? Who is lying to whom? What is the big Hollywood lie? And making a movie in Hollywood with new superstars, would that make it a documentary or a fiction film, a sort of cinema-lie?

Varda also lists twenty meanings for the film, all true, all limited.

In the lush garden behind a Hollywood home, the final moments of "The Beard" are passionately acted out. The gentle Viva is a shrieking Harlow in pink boa and dark green tights of overlapping leaves, James Rado a scowling, hysterical Billy the Kid in dark

Stetson, buckskin-fringed jacket and boots. They rip each other up verbally in a vicious climax!

The audience in the garden applaud the actors in their midst . . .

In their enormous opulent bed, Viva, Jerome Ragni and James Rado, three beautiful animals lean and graceful as cats, paw each other, rumple each other's manes. Viva is outrageously blase, James Rado ingenuously handsome, Jerry Ragni an uninhibited, cuddly bear. They act out "The Beard" love scenes: Viva as Harlow, Rado as The Kid, Jerry Ragni trying all the roles.

All, wearily: "Let's go to bed." They don't.

Viva murmurs seriously: "Our love is getting stale. I can no longer stand the lie of being actors, and being in love. It's all publicity . . . How can we love? . . . We are stars! . . . "

A collage of moviestars: movie posters, flashbulbs!, pink star in the Julie Andrews STAR poster, flashbulbs!, Telstar, stars on the flag, flashbulb!, Hollywood Boulevard stars, flashbulb!, sheriff's badge . . .

Nude, Viva floats on a mattress in the bright blue pool, surrounded by the garden's lush green jungle. The heads of Jim and Jerry pop from the water again and again, like a water ballet, their long scruffy hair eerily dry (it's filmed backwards) — Jim smiles, blonde and cool and reserved, while Jerry grins impishly below his tangle of dark. Viva reads a fan magazine to the scrawny pair: "Frank, despite his toughness, was shaken up by the news that Mia . . . " When she stops, the boys improvise nonsense verse, or Jerry spurts water. Viva cries, her voice cracking: "How do you love me?"

Jim: "Let me count the ways!"

Jerry: "Let me count the waves." (He splashes around.)

Viva: "How much to you love me?"

Jim: "Like three Empire State Buildings!"

"Live five Afghan hounds!"

"One Sequoia!"

"Ten Mac's Kansas City steaks!"

"Twenty-seven Bach concerts!"

"A thousand and one Arabian nights!"

"Two thousand and one California nights!" . . .

From a car traveling through Los Angeles, we see the garish airless landscape of that city: drive-in restaurants, gas stations, New England-cottage banks, supermarkets. A nervous mature female voice tells Viva, all offscreen: "I may look better but I haven't really recovered yet."

"All you need is a nice little shock," Viva prescribes. "I'll keep my clothes on all through your picture."

"Don't count your chickens, the deal isn't signed."

"So? If we don't make the movie, at least you'll get a suntan."

In the luxurious house's livingroom-bedroom, Shirley Clarke, the tense woman in her early forties, sees male boots: "Who is he?"

Viva is framed against the bright pool and garden: "*He*? You mean *they*. It's the same old happy traditional eternal triangle. The perfect end product of centuries of Western depravity. We get so bored being free and physical and liberated that we really must look for something else — "

"*That's* new."

"It sure is. I can't take any more of that emancipation crap," Viva sighs.

"The generation gap plus five hours on a plane plus two months of insomnia . . . it's too much, I'm flaked out. Save the rest of your theory until later." Shirley lies down on the big bed, the screen goes dark . . .

Shirley wakes. Jim and Jerry are dressed, on the terrace. Shirley is fascinated by the banana tree outside. Recognizing her, the two camp around, wear funny glasses, do a partial strip.

"They're trying to get into your new movie," Viva warns, "Pay no attention to them. Competitive bastards!"

"Seriously now," Jerry soothes, "Viva says you want to make a documentary about Hollywood. *Cinema verite* stuff. Well, we are Hollywood. Look at Jim. He gets around 20,000 kids to watch everytime he unzips his fly."

"Cut the bullshit," Jim warns.

"The point is," Viva sighs, "they come to see the myth, the legend, history, whatever makes a star."

"They haven't really accepted the idea," Shirley confides. "*They like* real screenplays, *they like* complete shooting scripts, with master shots, closeups, the whole bit. I may not get the deal after all. But if I do, I'll start thinking about Hollywood and looking around for stars and landmarks."

The three do an instant Hollywood routine, Jim declaiming: "In this kingdom, the Princes are sick. They must fight fire with fire, decadence with decadence, we must search for the mystical truth of love . . . "

Jerry stands before moviestar posters . . .

Poster of Cheshire cat: (Jerry makes faces: "We're all made here!")

Poster of Tiny Tim: (Jerry prays: "God Bless Tiny Tim!")

More posters . . .

A quick collage, beginning with a scene from "Hair," where the performers, Jerry among them, start undressing. Shot: Name plates on Aquarius Theatre wall; a screaming audience at a Doors concert, Jim visible; Klieg lights, celebrities, mobs at a Hollywood premiere . . .

In the livingroom-bedroom, the three stir and wake. They exchange good morning kisses, then agree someone must make coffee:

"Go or I'll whip you with my hair!"

"Go or I'll get under the sheet and stay there for hours!"

Viva complains: "I mean, like competition is ruining this trip. We three should strive for the real deep feeling of love. Each one should learn to be devoted to the others. To bring coffee is the first conscious gesture of marital love. Who's going?"

"It's tradition!" Jim argues. "The wife is the first to rise and she returns to bed with the breakfast tray. I've seen it in a million movies!"

Viva: "But then the husband goes out into the world and brings home the bacon. No one but me brings home *my* bacon. I'm not the traditional wife. It's all wrong. Let's try it some other way."

"Married life is getting out of hand already," Jerry states. "Let's go back to our world and make love."

"There goes coffee."

"Make love, not coffee . . . "

In the kitchen, all make coffee in different stages of undress. Shirley enters, dressed for business: "What have you been up to?"

Jerry: "Hollywood Year Zero. This could be the start of something small."

"I told you there was a subject for you right here," Viva exclaims. "Follow us from uninhibited sexual freedom to the brave new world of feeling."

"And watch me leap from the world of *cinema* to the Hollywood jungle," Shirley responds. "Bring on the Big Knife!" . . .

Again we see Los Angeles from a moving car. Shirley ponders her presentation to the producers, reflects on the city's cruel light versus the grime and noise of Manhattan, recalls a recent private crisis. Tormented, she watches the giant letters H O L L Y W O O D atop the Hollywood Hills . . .

All have lunch on a coffee shop terrace, Viva and Jerry at ease, Jim disturbed, looking trapped when a teenybopper sashays over for his autograph. Viva declares breathlessly: "He is *the* most."

Jerry: "For those under eighteen."

Viva choruses: "We love you, Jim Morrison, we all do!"

A group approaches which includes Shirley and Carlos, a dark thoughtful young man, introduced as the writer of *Horror Movies*, and a specialist on films of the 1920s and 1930s.

"How was your meeting?"

Shirley thinks it was pretty vague: "They're scared, they don't trust me, they don't even know my work and they don't care to. So we try to sell them a thrill. If they believe they can make money from it, they'll buy me . . . "

In a Hollywood office, well-dressed lawyers and agents discuss a project professionally: percentages, subsidiary rights, mutual agreements, censorship problems, rights to the final cut, domestic grosses, and so on. There is never a word about the subject of the film, or the talent of the director . . .

In the bedroom, Viva wears a feathered dishabille, Jim and Jerry are draped in bath towels like Roman senators. They look high. The room itself is a shambles, the great bed unmade, the pillows all around, the TV on with the sound low. Shirley comes in in a bullfighter's costume and turns on with them.

The three begin soap-boxing again. They persist that, although they don't look it, they're trying to get away from sex, to break the habit.

Love, Shirley tells them, is a choice dictated by passion, but this is too boring to explain. She adds that natural law opposes feeling, unless one decides feeling should rule nature.

A title: WHAT DO THEY WANT?

Jerry says their aim is to establish if feelings lead to eroticism.

Viva's is the quest for mystical love.

Jim wants to experience universal love through personal feelings, himself acting in the manner of a medium.

Shirley would just like the money to film them, to make a movie which would answer all these questions.

Viva, Jim and Jerry resolve to escape childhood and reach adulthood through the pains and joys of parenthood. They decide to put themselves through the Instant Family Test.

We see them in the bedroom. Shirley plays the TV louder. She wants the news announcements of the primary elections tomorrow . . .

In the livingroom-bedroom, Jim and Jerry enter with three neutral looking children — they introduce them to Viva:

The first child, 10, was borrowed against an autograph of Jim Morrison.

The second child, 5, has been loaned by a friend.

The third child, 1, has been entrusted to them by a hippy couple.

The morning with the children is a slapstick nightmare. The adults offer balloons, toys, food, drinks, games, the pool. The children are impossible; they refuse to take naps, urinate in the bright pool, eat nothing but french fries in catsup. At noon, Shirley calls to say things aren't working out for her. She can't come to lunch, the meeting is in the afternoon. The threesome give each child a sleeping pill, so they all expire on the big bed: "I think we've got to find another way to spiritual life . . . "

Collage: still photographs of child stars: Shirley Temple, Jane Withers, Jackie Coogan, Jackie Cooper, the Our Gang Kids . . .

While the children sleep, Viva, Jim, and Jerry transform

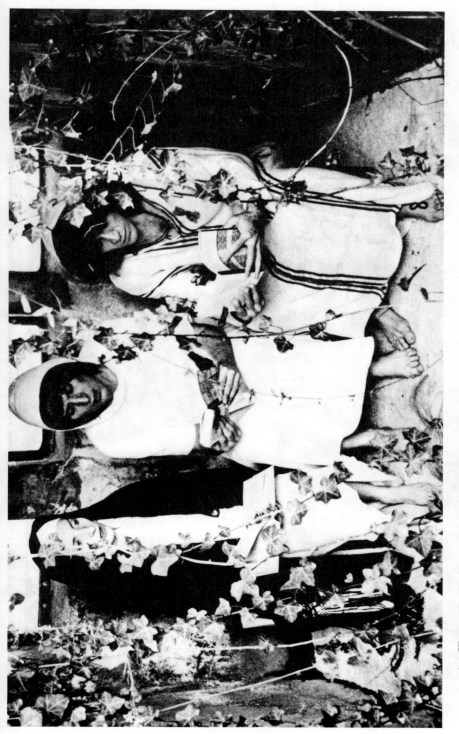

**Art History II: The lions as Mystical Three: Viva a stark Teresa of Avalon; Jim a St. John of the Cross; Jerry a St. Augustine, cowled, robed, pious-faced, hunched over religious paperbacks.**

Art History III: The lions as Picasso composition, shaped by Shirley Clarke's filmmaking skills.

Art History IV: The lions as pagan artist/muses, another Picasso composition, serious and unerotic.

themselves into the Mystical Three: Viva is a stark St. Teresa of Avalon, Jim becomes St. John of the Cross, Jerry is St. Augustine, all cowled and robed beneath ivy, expressions pious, hunched over religious paperbacks. Each reads from their writings in a sort of "mystical-verbal" collage . . .

We see a Hollywood office, but Shirley never appears. Again, agents and lawyers stuffily wrangle. The studio gets the upper hand, the deal is off, they don't trust Shirley's ideas. Off camera, she asks for the details . . .

In the livingroom-bedroom, a depressed Shirley finds a hasty note: "We've gone to return the little freaks."

Shirley lies down, browses in an equipment catalog, studies the banana tree in the bright outdoors. The camera composes shots of it, inside the "master" view from Shirley's perspective . . .

The same way, Shirley sets up compositions for Viva, Jim and Jerry, these making them figures in paintings. The compositions seem to derive from Picasso's drawings, making the three sexless arrangements of males and a female: Viva stretched bonily across Jerry's lap, Jim watching them, his back to the camera, a redundant censor. Shirley moves in and out of the frame, adjusting them. They speak a triple monologue: Jim a poem, Viva describing her feminine dreams, Jerry chanting. Shirley seems to be filming this, but from their point of view, it's only a paper cutout camera.

Cut: Shirley still lies on the big bed, always staring at the banana tree, composing more shots, as she cries softly . . .

A phone call: The three invite her to the party, but she won't go. She stares at the bright green garden from the dark bedroom.

Another nude Picasso composition of the Three: Jim sits writing on a board, Viva stands with flowers in her hair, Jerry plays the flute, all in sexless undress. The effect is un-erotic pagan seriousness. We hear pen on paper, flute, Viva humming softly.

On the bed, Shirley is crying.

A third composition: The backs of Jim and Jerry against a wallpaper wall of ivy on white bricks. Viva's leg and breast seem to be framed paintings hung on the wall: Life Deformed by Art.

Shirley has discovered a bottle of sleeping pills in the bedtable. But "This is not my style," she murmurs, and the filmmaker, Agnes Varda, herself, steps from behind the rolling camera to play the suicide scene . . .

Jim, Jerry and Viva return. They are upset by the double shooting of Andy Warhol and Bobby Kennedy. As they turn on the TV, they discover Shirley in the bedroom, seemingly asleep. With a joke they sit down to watch the news: the election, the shooting, hysterical people shouting while Bobby lies bleeding, all in bluish wavering images, three strange lovers peering at a different tragic strangeness.

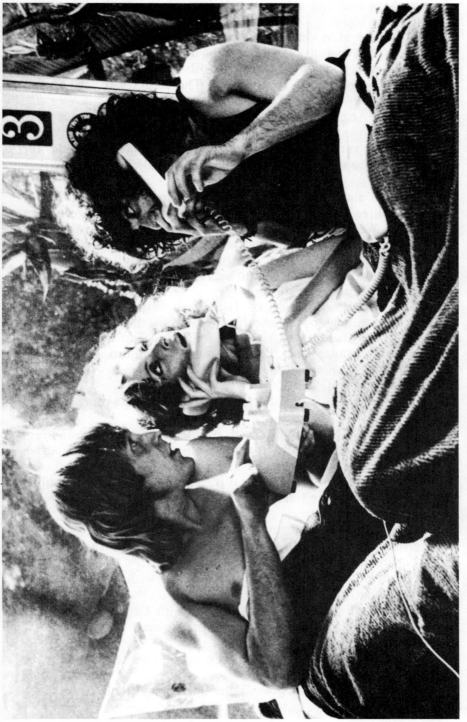

Art History VI: The lions as detached U.S. movie moguls in bed, watching Kennedy assassination as artistry.

An ambulance speeds towards the hospital. Leaving Shirley where she lies, Viva and Jim sleep next to her, while Jerry settles on the carpet for the night.

They wake at noon and find the bottle, realize Shirley is unconscious. The boys shake her and call a doctor, as Viva wails breathlessly that everybody is either shot or dying, that she should have cared more, is selfish, guilty, unhappy. The boys try to feed Shirley coffee.

The Los Angeles streets seen from a speeding vehicle: a siren screams along.

Viva, Jim and Jerry watch reruns of the election debacle, the commentator reports on his condition. Viva worries about Shirley, about Andy . . .

Viva, Jim and Jerry eat breakfast, watching a TV film of Bobby Kennedy's life. The implication is he is dead. Pierre Salinger makes statements. We see him swimming, shooting rapids in a kayak, full of life . . . The three comment that the Kennedys brought stardom to American life, became the *real* American superstars.

Viva calls, finds Shirley will be released the next day. Andy Warhol's condition still critical . . .

Andy Warhol's paintings of Jackie Kennedy, Marilyn Monroe. Behind them sounds of a nurse fussing with Shirley: "Get up, Shirley — do you feel like eating something? You must get something in you. Here's orange juice. Drink as much as you can. Look . . . it's here on the table . . . reach for it . . . or buzz me.

"Did Bobby win?"

"I can see we're feeling better, already. Yes, he won, but . . . "

"Good."

"Then you don't know about it. But how could you?" . . .

The Richy Herold exhibit, paintings strongly derived from pornographic postcards. Offscreen, Viva, Jerry and Jim comment on the pictures, talk to Herold himself. Viva repeats that Rick resembles Andy Warhol, she can't tell one from the other, or even who was shot, or where they are . . .

In the livingroom-bedroom, Shirley sits surrounded by pillows. Viva gives her a tray with food and flowers. Shirley: "You'd make a wonderful nurse."

"Part of my new program," Viva sighs. "I wish I didn't look so dreadful in white."

The doorbell rings, and Viva returns with Carlos, who suavely kisses Shirley and sits on the bed: "Darling, how are you?"

"Divine."

"You didn't even make the back page. Competition is fierce these days."

"I know . . . my timing was all wrong. Forget it. It all seems so

140

silly now."

Viva comes and goes. Carlos calls to her: "See what happens when she finally comes to Hollywood? You could have made your movie without leaving the Chelsea Hotel, with posters, stills, old records . . . "

"I wanted to shoot it *here*! To film the real Hollywood."

"How can you film a state of mind? The real Hollywood is pure nostalgia, not a place."

"I wanted to see the new breed, the old studios. It's all over, I'm not making my film anymore . . . "

"You mean I won't get to be the New Garbo," Viva moans, "the New Dietrich, the New Harlow, all rolled into one?"

Collage, Carlos comments over the images: The Walt Disney Studio Entrance, Paramount Gate, Columbia, Metro; The Larry Edmonds Bookshop of Cinema Memorabilia; Books, Posters, stills, rare documents; traveling shots of swimming pools, gardens, colonnades of old star homes. Carlos: "In 1930, the Paramount slogan was: 'More stars than there are in heaven.' . . . In '28, Pickfair was the Royal House of Mary Pickford and Douglas Fairbanks, here they received European aristocracy . . . "

In the empty swimming pool, Viva and Jim play again the roles of Harlow and Billy the Kid. Jerry plays Eternity, a bearded statue spouting water into the pool. The audience is composed of children sitting at the shallow end, drinking Coke, eating popcorn and ice cream, even smoking pot.

On the soundtrack, Viva, Jim, Jerry, Carlos and Shirley talk about the movies . . .

They all sit together on the floor, Indian-style, as the conversation goes on. Themes: You can write a poem and not publish it, the poem already exists; you can paint and not exhibit, the painting already exists; but film does not exist unless you shoot it . . .

Viva thinks that an actress who does not perform ceases to be an actress. Carlos says that Viva remains Viva whether she acts or not.

Shirley says that she sees them, not as stars, but as mythological figures, cannot help visualizing them out of reality . . .

Jim recites, how he keeps refusing parts because *they* always require him to play a singer, a sex symbol, a star, a cliche. He would like to play a real human character with real human problems, like wife and children, like a migrant worker or an elevator man, earning wages, getting fired . . .

Viva recites, how tired she feels of being used as a sexy nude freak. It's getting more and more difficult for her to get a real part. "I'd like to be in a real movie . . . I want to breathe!" She does only that.

Jerry too recites, spiraling steadily inward: "Hair" started as an

**141**

off-Broadway venture, is a Broadway show. Now Hollywood wants the movie rights, so any subversion in the play is about to be absorbed by the industry. Now is he sure he feels strongly against the system . . .

The livingroom-bedroom is neat and empty, the TV is on: The Kennedy funeral service at St. Patrick's Cathedral in New York City.

One by one they enter: Viva fixing her hair after a shower, Shirley from the kitchen whipping eggs, Jerry from the street with groceries, Jim from the pool. Shirley remarks that this real live spectacular is making voyeurs of them all, peeping Toms of history.

Viva is dressed in black.

Jim watches seriously . . .

Now they go about their everyday routines while watching the Kennedy special. Viva makes phone calls, shaves her legs. Jim reads, Jerry does pushups, Shirley watches the train carrying the funeral cortege. When several bystanders are killed by accident, Jim and Viva turn off the TV.

Viva, Jim and Jerry go to bed together. They're tired, warm, tender. Though they also crack "alone at last" jokes, it's clear they enjoy each other's presence and appreciate their fragile happiness. They hold each other tightly but chastely. They put out the light . . .

Views of Los Angeles from a moving car. All the cars have their lights on in full daylight, a gesture of mourning. We hear Viva, Jim, Jerry, Shirley on the way to the airport. They all wish Shirley better luck next time, comment on the lights. Shirley has the feeling that she made her Hollywood movie after all, even if it does not exist. It's like the headlights in the daytime, not real . . .

**Lion's Love** is one of the most sophisticated and hopeful views of America by a modern foreign director. Using some of Godard's devices, Varda goes far beyond his complex self-awareness as a filmmaker to explore Hollywood past and present, and the nature of acting itself in evoking American life.

The technique of the film has many similarities with the flat, eclectic, awareness-of-making-a-movie style of Godard's **Made in U.S.A.**: the use of single still picture, cartoons, posters, and collages; Pop art "comic strip shots," (e.g., Jerry and the Cheshire cat) and titles (e.g., WHAT DO THEY WANT?); in-jokes for film experts ("The Big Knife," "Hollywood, Year Zero"); philosophical discussions and metaphysical digression sequences; a self-conscious "quest" storyline (Shirley's deal) that evolves as it goes along, finally-failing-yet-succeeding. Hoops (7.3) has commented interestingly upon the last: "Each scene connects to what has gone before as its significance unfolds in the viewer's mind — no plot guides us. The point is to enjoy what is at hand."

This is not a true innovation, but the use of the thriller's technique of clues and red herrings becoming clear as the film goes on, transformed and extended for new artistic purposes. Likewise, Varda takes Godard's self-consciousness itself to its final Pirandellian limits when the creator replaces her persona in the suicide sequence.

Those dissatisfied with the film usually fault Godard's influence. Hoops concludes (7.3): "Agnes Varda throws herself into strange waters, where she struggles to appear composed while grasping desperately at the flotsam and jetsam of the wreck of the traditional film she has abandoned." Hoops concludes the film's pattern of contrivance and spontaneity gives it a certain tension, yet makes it ineffective as a serious work. Likewise, Molly Haskell (7.2) sees **Lion's Love** more as an entertainment, praising the directrix' visual style: "Precious brilliance and color intoxication . . . perfect for a life style which is all surface and sexiness." (7.2)

**Lion's Love** nevertheless explores several intersting ideas in serious and complex ways, though the treatment is so understated they're apt to slip by. First, of course, it deals with the new sexuality. Most "serious" films shy off from this problem, and even the foreign artists discussed tend to simplify the situation into tedious couples living together (Demy, Schlesinger), or one night stands of flower-child-innocence (Antonioni, Demy), or capitalistic corruption (Boorman, Schlesinger).

Varda goes beyond all these to create a sexy funloving *menage-a-trois*, a new love style living with mutual tenderness and pleasure. She comments: "To show conjugal love between three people, free and happy together, is to show a certain image of freedom in California. A threesome is a better combination than a couple if you care to show moral freedom. Especially, when the scabrous aspect is not used as such. It then becomes a widening of the concept of love." (7.6) Varda's previous **Le Bonheur** also dealt with a triple, though an unhappy one, and the theme of moment-to-moment living and joys in a sexually unconventional world runs through both works. **Lion's Love** has been praised by one woman's liberation writer as proof of the need for more women filmmakers, with their own approach to this topic. The problems of role assignment ("The wife is the first to rise — it's traditional!"), the problems of having children ("We've got to find another way to spiritual life . . . "), and "proving" one's love ("Like three Empire State Buildings!") are also touched on. The treatment, however, is so frothy one must pay close attention.

Another aspect of sexuality that is shyly and slyly dealt with in **Lion's Love** is the basic nature of sex itself. One notes that, despite spectacular advertising, almost all serious filmmakers today have maintained the "conventional" wisdom of Hollywood. Even the group discussed largely accept the old categories: domestic torpor (Demy, Forman), sado-masochistic violence (Boorman, Schlesinger),

**143**

romantic frenzy (Boorman, Demy, Schlesinger), free love (red "hippie"), innocence (Antonioni, Forman). Here again Varda plays with our basic ideas of sexuality by giving her mature triple of aesthetic sybarites total freedom — they suggest various relations between the sex urge, eroticism itself, and feelings. These are only proposed (Hollywood doesn't buy it), but suggests some problems of life after the Revolutions of Antonioni and Godard, the complete corruption of Boorman and Schlesinger, or the hippie slough of Demy and Forman. The real filmic exploration of sex, Varda suggests, has hardly begun, least of all in the pornography of Times Square.

A reflection of the complex treatment of acting in **Lion's Love** is the very American idea of existence as a spectator, as part of an audience. The film shows a bloody murder (Bobby Kennedy), and funeral, a suicide attempt (Shirley), the heroes kidding around and sleeping next to what seems to be a corpse, casual appropriation and drugging of children, yet none of this assorted slaughter, mayhem and voyeurism seems to matter much. The spectator's "liberation" is brought about by an assortment of factors: the characters' own blase attitudes, constant undercutting of the film's versimilitude, the lack of dramatic "preparation"; the ambiance of carefree narcissism. Several speculations follow: Do aspects of modern American life — politics, social conventions, etc., promote such attitudes towards each other? Is this "levelling" in the film only a special case of the very limited U.S. responses made even to successful entertainment and art? Are the characters' performances more and more overt displays of the limitations modern artists hide, even from themselves?

Varda ended one interview (7.6) by suggesting how **Lion's Love** for her reflects American life today. She states she tried to break the sentimental pattern of old movies about Hollywood, where the town buys you out: "In my film, they don't care. They want to be actors, they want to be famous, Jerry, Jim, and Viva, they want to be famous — but on the other hand, they don't care, Hollywood won't break them, they'll live their lives. They don't play the game of Hollywood.

". . . They want something else. It's a new breed of becoming successful. Which means, my film deals with NOW. There is a new way of living in America, even in Show Biz there is a new way of being free. Everybody wants to become successful in America. But in so many different ways. And I think it's interesting to oppose all these ways and to look into contradictions. I have always been interested in contradictions. You put them together, all the contradictions, and there is a short circuit. I am interested in short circuits . . .

"Let me put it this way: I've been much more surprised with America from going to Los Angeles than from being in New York. I have been raped there of my usual way of thinking, and my usual contradictions."

# Film Credits

ZABRISKIE POINT, U.S.A., 1969. Directed by Michelangelo Antonioni; produced by Carlo Ponti; screenplay by Michelangelo Antonioni, Fred Gardner, Sam Shepard, Tonio Guerra and Clare Paploe; photographed by Alfio Contini; music by The Pink Floyd, Kaleidoscope, The Rolling Stones, Patti Page and others; editing assistant, Franco Arcalli. With Mark Frechette, Daria Halprin, Rod Taylor, Kathleen Cleaver and The Open Theatre of Joe Chalkin, Panavision and Metrocolor. Distributed in 35mm by Metro-Goldwyn-Mayer. Running time: 110 minutes.

POINT BLANK, U.S.A., 1967. Directed by John Boorman; produced by Judd Bernard and Robert Chartoff; screenplay by Alexander Jacobs and David and Rafe Newhouse, based on the novel "The Hunter" by Richard Stark; a Judd Bernard-Irwin Winkler production released by Metro-Goldwyn-Mayer. With Lee Marvin — Walker, Angie Dickinson — Chris, Keenan Wynn — Yost, Caroll O'Connor — Brewster, Lloyd Bochner — Frederick Carter, Michal Strong — Stegman, John Vernon — Mal Reese, Sharon Acker — Lynne. Running time: 92 minutes.

THE MODEL SHOP, U.S.A., 1968. Written and directed by Jacques Demy, based on original idea by Demy; produced by Jacques Demy. English dialogue by Adrien Joyce. Camera (Perfect Color), Michel Hugo; editor, Walter Thompson; production designer, Kenneth A. Reid; songs composed and performed by Spirit; sound, Les Fresholtz, Arthur Piantadosi; assistant director, Herbert Willis. Columbia Pictures release. Screened at Columbia home office January 7, 1969. With Anouk Aimée — Lola, Gary Lockwood — George Matthews, Alexandra Hay — Gloria, Carol Cole — Barbara, Severn Darden — Portly Man, Tom Fielding — Gerry, Neil Elliot — Fred, Jacqueline Miller — Model No. 1, Anne Randall — Model No. 2, Duke Hobbs — David, Craig Littler — Rob, Jeanne Sorel — Secretary, Jon Lawson — Tony. Running time: 90 minutes.

**TAKING OFF**, U.S.A., 1971. Directed by Milos Forman; produced by Alfred W. Crown, associate producer, Michael Hausman; written by Milos Forman, John Guare, Jean-Claude Carriere and John Klein. Color by Movielab. A Forman-Crown-Hausman production in association with Claude Berri. Released by Universal. With Lynn Carlin — Lynn Tyne, Buck Henry — Larry Tyne, Linnea Heacock — Jeannie Tyne, Georgia Engel — Margot, Tony Harvey — Tony, Audra Lindley — Ann Lockston, Paul Benedict — Ben Lockston, Vincent Schiavelli, David Gittler, the Ike and Tina Turner Revue. Running time: 93 minutes.

**MADE IN U.S.A.**, U.S.A., 1967. Written and directed by Jean-Luc Godard; Camera (Eastmancolor), Raoul Coutard; editor, Agnes Giulemot. Previewed in Paris. Athos release of Rome-Paris Films, Anouchka Films production. With Anna Karina — Paula Nelson, Laszlo Szabo — Richard Widmark, Jean-Pierre Leaud — Donald Siegel, Yves Alfonso — David Goode, Kyoko Kosaka — Doris Mizoguchi, Herself — Marianne Faithful. Running time: 85 minutes.

**MIDNIGHT COWBOY**, U.S.A., 1969. Directed by John Schlesinger. Screenplay by Waldo Salt based on the novel of James Leo Herlihy. Camera (Technicolor), Adam Holdender; design, John Robert Lloyd; editor, Hugh A. Robertson; music supervision, John Barry. United Artists release of Jerome Hellman-John Schlesinger production. With Dustin Hoffman — Ratso, Jon Voight — Joe Buck, Sylvia Miles — Cass, John McGiver — O'Daniel, Brenda Vaccaro — Shirley, Bernard Hughes — Towny, Ruth White — Sally Buck, Jennifer Salt — Annie, Gil Rankin — Woodsy Niles, T. Tom Marlow — Little Joe — — Gary Owens, George Eppersen — Ralph, Al Scott — Cafeteria Manager, Linda Davis — Mother on the Bus, J.T. Masters — Old Cow-Hand, Arlene Reeder — The Old Lady, Georgann Johnson — Rich Lady, Jonathan Kramer — Jackie, Anthony Holland — TV Bishop, Bob Balaban — The Young Student, Jan Tice — Freaked-Out Lady, Paul Benjamin — Bartender, Peter Scalia, Vito Siracuse — Grocers, Peter Zamagias — Hat Shop Owner, Arthur Anderson — Hotel Clerk, Tina Scala, Alma Felix — Laundromat Ladies, Richard Clarke — Escort Service Man, Ann Thomas — The Frantic Lady, Joan Murphy — The Waitress, Al Stetson — Bus Driver, Viva — Gretel McAlbertson, Gastone Rossilli — Hansel McAlbertson. Others: Ultra Violet, Paul Jabara, International Velvet, William Dorr, Cecelia Lipson, Taylor Mead, Paul Morrissey. Running time: 119 minutes.

**LION'S LOVE**, U.S.A., 1970. Directed by Agnes Varda, Executive producer, Max L. Raab; produced by Agnes Varda. Written by Agnes Varda. Camera (Technicolor) Stefan Larner; editor, Robert Dalva; music, Joseph Byrd; art direction, Jack Wright, III; sound, George Arch, Andy Babbish; historical material, Carlos Clarons. With Viva, Jerome Ragni, James Rado, Shirley Clarke, Carlos Clarens and Eddie Constantine. Also appearing in a scene from "The Beard" by Michael McClure are Billie Dixon and Richard Bright. Running time: 115 minutes.

# Addendum

# Foreign Filmmakers
# on America:  A Filmography

The following is acknowledged to be a tentative and necessarily incomplete list of significant, notable or exemplary films by foreign filmmakers on aspects of life in the United States. In explanation, I would point out that the research problems involved are so vast — from an understanding of foreign cultural contexts of works to limited-release of films to the loss of older works — that this can only be a first approximation of such a list. (In passing, any help, foreign or domestic, would be appreciated towards revisions for later editions.) Clearly, the subject may be pursued in several directions:

- works of foreign expatriates (the von Stroheim, Lang, Hitchcock, Schlesinger and Wenders generations).
- foreign treatments of U.S. genres (included here are such exemplars as spaghetti westerns, crime thrillers, and classic novels).
- aesthetically interesting propaganda (see Erik Barnouw's very complete treatment of anti-U.S. propaganda during the Vietnam War in his *Documentary*).
- even works of very alienated U.S. ethnics (e.g., perhaps **Sweet Sweetback**, by Melvin van Peebles, should be included here).

*List Nomenclature:*

The creator's name, nation, and film release year immediately follow the title in English. D = director, W = writer, P = producer, b/o = based on, L = loan. Many of the films listed are available in 16mm, and I have listed sources for the short factual ones. The programmer should check out the standard commercial film rental catalogs and, if these fail, consult such sources as Goethe House in New York City.

**A VIEW OF THE WRECK OF THE MAINE.** W, P, D: Georges Méliès, French, 1898. Ingeniously reconstructed newsreel of U.S. intervention in Cuba. Also, **Divers at Work on the Wreck of the**

**Maine** (no date), and **Mishaps of the N.Y.—Paris Race** (no date), sarcastic travelogue of an actual race organized by a U.S. company. Méliès' brother Gaston also shot several short subjects in America.

**TONTOLINI AND THE AMERICAN COUSIN.** W, D: Ferdinand Guillaume, Italian, 1911. P: Cines. L: Museum of Modern Art. Guillaume, an Italian comic actor, is mistaken for a long-absent cousin, thought made eccentric by a visit to the U.S.

**MAX AND THE CLUTCHING HAND.** W, D: Max Linder, French, 1915. D: Pathé. The French comedian's glorious spoof of U.S. serials, particularly those of Pearl White.

**FOOLISH WIVES.** W,D: Erich von Stroheim, Austrian, 1922. P: Universal Motion Pictures. C: Stroheim, Mae Busch, Maude George. L: Museum of Modern Art. Classic film of gullible upper-class Americans, visiting and seduced by decayed aristocrats of Europe.

**AN EYE FOR AN EYE.** D: A. Litvinov, Soviet Russian, 1924. P: AFKU. Thriller about U.S. spies who try to steal a new Soviet war gas.

**EXTRAORDINARY ADVENTURES OF MR. WEST IN BOLSHE-VIKLAND.** D: Lev Kuleshov, Soviet Russian, 1924. C: V. Pudovkin, B. Barnet, A. Kokhlava. L: Museum of Modern Art. Comic-satirical cowboy film. Due to U.S. Senator West's misunderstanding Soviet life, he hires a cowboy to protect him from "uncivilized" Soviets, who he imagines resemble Hollywood Indians. On arrival, he's outwitted by counter-revolutionaries for most of the film.

**GREED.** W, D: Erich von Stroheim, Austrian, 1925. b/o novel *Greed* by Frank Norris. P: MGM. C: Gibson Gowland, Zazu Pitts. American lower class rendered as beasts at the mercy of heredity and environment, in an elaborately detailed treatment of the period.

**MISS MEND.** D: B. Barnet and F. Ozep, Soviet Russians, 1926. P: Mezhrappom. "Red detective" thriller set in U.S., resembling American genre films. Three left wing reporters and their girlfriend seek to expose crimes of a villainous capitalist. Highly popular in the Soviet Union.

**THE SCARLET LETTER.** D: Victor Sjöstrom, Swedish, 1926. W: S.W. Francis Marion, b/o W. Hawthorne novel. P: MGM. C: Lillian Gish, Lars Hanson, Henry B. Waltham. Gish intuited, correctly, that Sjostrom's temperament was closer to Hawthorne's than contemporaneous Americans.

**SUSPICIOUS LUGGAGE.** D: Girgori Grichin, Soviet Russian, 1926. P: VUFKU. In this light satire, a Soviet traveler in the U.S. carrying a box of oranges has his luggage mistaken for a box of poison gas containers by the bourgeois police.

**THE UNVANQUISHED.** D: A. Isordium, Soviet Russian, 1927. W: L. Knazhinski. P: VUFKU. Drama of U.S. class struggle and workers' movement, criticized in the Soviet Union as far from U.S. realities.

**CANNONS OR TRACTORS.** W, P, D: Esther Shub, Soviet Russian, 1930. Compilation documentary contrasting U.S. capitalism (e.g., a bishop christens a warship: peace on earth good will to men!) with the U.S.S.R.'s new civilization (industrialization scenes titled: The Five Year Plan succeeding in four!).

**MISTRESS OF A FOREIGNER.** D. Kenji Mizoguchi, Japanese, 1930. W: Hatamoto. P: Nikkatsu. Story of poor girl in 19th century Japan, who is trained in traditional arts, becomes a geisha, then, against her will, becomes mistress of U.S. consul Townsend Harris, who forces her lover to give her up.

**JIMMIE HIGGINS.** D. Giorgi Tasin, Soviet Russian, 1931. S: Isaak Babel, b/o Upton Sinclair novel. P: VUFKA. C: Amvrosi Buchma. Young U.S. soldier, already a victim of capitalism and fighting in the 1919 Soviet Intervention, realizes Communism suits him best.

**BLACK AND WHITE.** D: Langston Hughes, Soviet Russian production, 1932. Reportedly unfinished film on U.S. prejudice, involving steelmill union man who tries to hire blacks, but is opposed by poor, managers, and capitalists. A Birmingham race riot leads to radio pleas to northern liberals, who do nothing, and northern union men, who bus to Alabama "to save their Negro brothers." Project cancelled on F.D.R. election.

**JOBS AND MEN.** D: A. Macheret, Soviet Russian, 1932. P: Soyuz-kino-Moscow. Melodrama involving conflict of views between a Soviet worker and U.S. technician on Dnieper dam project, symbolizing the Soviet Union's urge to surpass U.S.

**MORRIS MAKES HIS FORTUNE.** German, 1932. P: Monopol Films. C: Siegfried Arno, Dorothea Diessle. Merry musical of Berlin salesman betrothed in New York City to U.S. millionaire's long-lost daughter. In one hilarious incident, he imitates a blackfaced singer at a models' ball.

**RETURN OF NATHAN BECKER**. D: B.V. Shipiss, R.M. Milman, Soviet Russian, 1935. P: Belgoshkino Prod. C: David Gutman, S.M. Mikhoels. Bricklayer-protagonist returns to his village after 28 years in the U.S., together with a U.S. black friend. After misundertandings, the Soviets decide a combination of U.S. and Soviet work methods is best.

**CIRCUS**. D: Grigori Alexandrov, Soviet Russian, 1936. P: Mosfilm. Musical comedy laced with propaganda, featuring a U.S. woman who flees to the Soviet Union to escape racial bigotry.

**THE FUGITIVE FROM CHICAGO**. D: Johannes Meyer, Bavaria, 1936. C: G. Froehlich, H. VonMeyerinck. An honest young German emigrant returns home, and perks up a failing auto factory in the U.S. style.

**FURY**. D: Fritz Lang, German, 1933. W: Barlett Cormack. P: J. Mankiewicz for MGM. C: Spencer Tracy, Sylvia Sidney, Walter Brennan. Lang's first U.S. film — a classic study of U.S. mob violence.

**THE GHOST GOES WEST**. D: Rene Clair, French, 1936. W: Robert Sherwood. C: Robert Donat, Eugene Pallete. A rich U.S. citizen purchases an old ghost-ridden Irish castle, which is rebuilt in Sunnymede, Florida, with comic results.

**THE EMPEROR OF CALIFORNIA**. D, P: Luis Trencer, German, 1937. C: V. von Belasko. Dramatization of life of Swiss-American J.A. Sutter, whose life was destroyed in 1849 Goldrush and who dies on the Capitol steps in Washington, DC, still demanding justice.

**PUNKS ARRIVES FROM AMERICA**. K.H. Martin, German, 1937. P: UFA Prod. C: Lien Deyers, Sybelle Schmitz. Young German emigrant, now rich, returns home in disguise, to learn how his "failure" will be received.

**TALES OF MANHATTAN**. W, D: Julien Duvivier, French, 1937. W: Mr. Duvivier et al. P: 20th Century-Fox. C: Charles Boyer, Rita Hayworth, Paul Robeson. Story of a tail coat, as its covers shoulders of those in various walks of life. Includes disputed Negro episode.

**A YANK AT OXFORD**. D: Jack Conway, English, 1938. W: M.S. Boylan. P: Michael Balson. C: Robert Taylor, Vivien Leigh, Lionel Barrymore. Exemplifies British films of this period which cater to U.S. audiences, in this case via the nostalgia for a solid, innocent family.

**WITHOUT A HOPE**. D: Alexander Martin, Polish-Yiddish, 1939. b/o play "Ahn a Helm" by Jacob Cordin. P: Adolph Mann. C: Ida Haminska, Alexander Marten. Jewish immigrant-wife's hope of a new U.S. home is balked by her husband's temporary infatuation for a husky cabaret dancer.

**THE CANTOR'S SON**. D: Ilya Motyleff, Polish, 1940. W. Louis Friendman. C: Moishe Oysher, Forence Weiss. L: Audio-Brando-Contemporary. A Hebrew youth leaves Poland, builds a theatrical career in the U.S., but returns to the old country.

**OIL**. Argentian, 1941. C: Sebastian Chiola. A suave North American arrives to con the Argentinians out of their oil wells, but a local gent and an oilman's daughter outwit the American.

**HOLD BACK THE DAWN**. W, D: Billy Wilder, German, 1941. P: Universal Motion Pictures. C: Charles Boyer. An international charmer marries an old maid U.S. schoolteacher to escape Mexico — a sly comment on the period's U.S. quota on refugees from Europe.

**MR. ROOSEVELT CHANTS**. Nazi Germany, 1942. Reputed Nazi propaganda short with "a murky brand of anti-Semitism and anti-capitalism." A second short of this type was reputedly titled **Around the Statue of Liberty** (1943).

**SHADOW OF A DOUBT**. D: Alfred Hitchcock, British, 1943. W: Thornton Wilder et al. P: J.H. Skirball. C: Joseph Cotten, Teresa Wright. A particularly harsh vision of an American family — flawed, weak, prone to corruption and madness due to economic stress.

**THE SOUTHERNER**. W, D: Jean Renor, French, 1945. b/o G.S. Perry's novel *Hold Autumn in Your Hand*. C: Zachary Scott, Betty Feild. Forthright, sympathetic treatment of U.S. sharecroppers.

**A MATTER OF LIFE AND DEATH** (U.S. title: **STAIRWAY TO HEAVEN**). W, D, P: Michael Powell & F. Pressburger, British, 1946. C: David Niven, Kim Hunter, Raymond Massey. Heavenly allegory advocating greater U.S.-British unity, a theme that is present in **Journey Together** (1945), **A Canterbury Tale** (1944), **The Way to the Stars** (1945), and the James Bond films.

**VICTORY OF WOMEN**. D: Kenji Okichi, Japanese, 1946. W: Kogonopa & K. Shindo. P: Shochinnku. Clear assimilation of U.S. occupation ideas on female emancipation in story of professional women in law courts.

**A YANK IN LONDON.** D, W, P: Maurice Cowman, British, 1946. C: Rex Harrison, Dean Jagger. Romance of an American soldier and titled blonde beauty, suggesting British-U.S. differences all petty misunderstandings of each others' customs and habits.

**MONTE CASSINO.** D, P: Auturo Gemmiti, Italian, 1948. W: Mr. Gemmiti, et al. C: A.A. Lolli, V. Lay. Italian treatment of assault on Mt. Cassino in October, 1943 by General Mark Clark.

**NO ORCHIDS FOR MISS BLADISH.** D: John L. Cowles, British, 1948. P: A.R. Shipman. W: Mr. Cowles, b/o novel by J.H. Chase. C: Jack Laruge, Hugh McDermott. "As a supposed American gangster film, this touches bottom in sadism, morbidity, and taste" — *Variety*. "A disgrace to British films!" — *London Evening Standard*.

**PAISAN** (tr: "Buddy"). D, P: Roberto Rossellini, Italian, 1948. W: Federico Fellini, et al. C: Carmela Sazio, Robert von Loon, Six powerful dramatic incidents during the Italian campaign, emphasizing the problems of Allied understanding, with two involving American soldiers.

**THE RUSSIAN QUESTION.** D: Mikhail Romm, Soviet Russian, 1948. W: b/o novel by Konstantin Siminov. P: Mosfilm. A U.S. journalist traveling in Russia learns the Soviets are not war-mongers. At home, he's persecuted by press and government, loses his wife and house, and finally declares: "America's enemies are not in the Soviet Union, but in Washington!"

**THE BIG DAY.** W, D: Jaques Tati, French, 1950. C: Mr. Tati. A village postman sees a documentary on the advanced U.S. postal system, and takes off to create a comic French counterpart.

**MEETING ON THE ELBE.** D: Grigori Alexandrov, Soviet Russian, 1950. In a tense divided Germany, Americans work with ex-Nazis.

**SECRET MISSION.** D: Mikhail Romm, Soviet Russian, 1950. U.S. generals league with Hitler and Himmler to attack the Soviet Union at the end of World War II.

**THEY HAVE A COUNTRY.** D: Alexander Feinzimmer, Soviet Russian, 1950. Americans treat homeless war orphans as slaves, and bring them up to be anti-Russian fascists.

**WITHOUT PITY.** D: Alberto Lattuda, Italian, 1950. W: Federico Fellini & Tullio Pinelli. Black marketeers and the U.S. Army hound a black G.I. and his Italian girl, in a portrayal of life-after-dark relations between U.S. occupation troops and prostitutes.

**ANGELO.** W, D: Francesco de Roberts, Italian, 1951. P: Scalera Films. Story of a G.I. and Italian girl's offspring, all three treated as victims of circumstance.

**IN PEACETIME.** D: Vladimir Braun, Soviet Russian, 1951. Cold War drama in which U.S. submarine lays mines on Soviet shipping lanes, then tries to rescue a Soviet sub damaged by the mines, but is sunk by a Soviet warship.

**NATIVE SON.** D: Pierre Chenal, French, 1951. W: Richard Wright, b/o his novel. C: Gloria Maobon, Richard Wright. Filmed in Argentina, a careful but ineffective effort to realize the 1940s novel's portrayal of U.S. racism.

**THE HIJACKING.** D: Jan Kadar & Elmar Klos, Czechoslovakian, 1952. A Czech airliner, hijacked by the U.S. "C.I.C." to West Germany, fails to lead to defections by loyal Czech Communists. U.S. "arguments" include visits to sexy night clubs, bombing raid atrocity photographs, and torture — a Soviet counterpart of the U.S. **Man on a String.**

**SILVER DUST.** D: Abram Room, Soviet Russian, 1953. b/o August Yakobsin's novel *Jackals*. P: Mosfilm. U.S. black Communist and five other Americans, falsely jailed in U.S., are used in chemical warfare tests. Recued, they vow their jailers will one day face a people's court.

**THE THICK WALLED ROOM.** D: Masaki Kobayashi, Japanese, 1953. W: Kobo Abe, b/o diaries of war crimes prisoners. P: Sinei Productions. Very strong protest film against political and social injustice, showing those convicted were often forced into criminal acts by wartime superiors who went free. Emphasis on overall effects of war, including Japanese torturing of American prisoners of war, and how U.S. occupation leads a Japanese woman into prostitution.

**AMERICAN FARMERS VISIT RUSSIA.** D: Ztuzova, Soviet Russian, 1955. W: E. Kriger. P: Central Documentary Film Studio, Moscow. "Twelve Americans royally welcomed everywhere, inspect Odessa's wheatfields, and sing 'Old MacDonald' on boatride to Stalingrad." — N.Y. Times.

**RECORD OF A LIVING BEING.** D: Akira Kurasawa, Japanese, 1955. P: Toho. Contemporary drama of one man's fear of the U.S. atomic bomb, and his attempt to save himself.

**THERE'S ALWAYS TOMORROW.** D: Douglas Sirk, German, 1955. W: Bernard Schoenfield. P: Universal. C: Barbara Stanwyck, Fred Macmurray. Sirk's U.S. films deal mainly with unfulfilled lives of middle class Americans. In this case, a prosperous businessman, neglected by wife and family, meets an old love, and becomes aware of his own miserable situation.

**REACH FOR THE SKY.** D: Lewis Gilbert, British. W: Mr. Gilbert, et al. P: Pinnacle Films. C: Kenneth More, Muriel Pavlow. Biography of neurotic U.S. military hero who wins the Victoria Cross.

**BLACK RIVER.** D: Masaki Kobayashi, Japanese, 1957. W: Zeno Matsuyama. P: Shochiku. Expose of corruption around U.S. bases in postwar Japan, blaming Japanese social system for allowing prostitutes, gamblers, and gangsters to prey on U.S. soldiers.

**CITY OF GOLD.** Colin Low and Wolf Koenig, Canadian, 1957. W: Pierre Berton. Period photography used to reconstruct Alaskan Gold Rush. "More sense of gold fever . . . than dozens of Hollywood epics" — Pauline Kael.

**THE MEXICAN.** D, P: V. Kaplunovsky, Soviet Russian, 1957. W: W.E. Raginsky, b/o Jack London novel. P: Artkino. Russian rendering of Los Angeles ghetto, in which a Mexican prizefighter earns money for the anti-Diaz forces in the ring.

**RAID ON THE DOPE RING.** D: Henry Decoin, French, 1957. C: Jean Gabin, Lila Kedrova. French counterpart of U.S. 1930s crime thriller, with "strange accents, more refined sadistic and erotic habits, and a whole new . . . exotic gangster argot." — Pauline Kael.

**AUNT FROM CHICAGO.** D: Alekos Salekarios, Greek, 1959. C: Orestic Makris, Georgia Vassiadou. A comedy in which a Coptic aunt returns from America, and rescues her neices from spinsterhood via bikinis and other U.S. salespersonship.

**THE BATTLE OF THE SEXES.** D: Charles Crichton, British, 1959. W: M. Danischewsky, b/o James Thurber novel. C: Peter Sellers, Constance Cummings, Robert Morley. A traditionalist Scottish textile mill hires a U.S. efficiency expert; British anti-Americanism suggested by locals' resentment of progress.

**I WANT TO BE A SHELLFISH**. D: S. Hashimoto, Japanese, 1959. b/o works of Tetsutaro Kato. P: Tho International. C: Furanki, Sakai Michiyo, Aratama. Powerful, understated story of Japanese condemned to death as a war criminal on a technicality, portraying the last days of his imprisonment by the Americans.

**THE MOUSE THAT ROARED**. D: Jack Arnold, British, 1959. W: Roger McDougall & Stanley Mann. P: Walter Shenson. C: Peter Sellers, Jean Seberg. Comedy of small country that declares war on U.S. in expectation of being quickly defeated, then refurbished via U.S. aid.

**TWO MEN IN MANHATTAN**. W, D: Jean Pierre Melville, French, 1959. P: Columbia Pictures. C: Pierre Grasett, Jean Daracante. Slick manhunt in New York City involving a U.N. diplomat. Notable for bits of Americana, and director's fascination with dark urban criminal universe in an American context.

**BREATHLESS**. W, D & P: Jean-Luc Godard, French, 1960. C: J.P. Belmondo, Jean Seberg. The thriller's Jean Seberg character has been called the ultimate 1950s American girl in Paris (a brainless bitch who betrays her criminal lover), while Belmondo's charming crook is a totally "Americanized" Frenchman. Part of the French New Wave.

**I SPIT ON YOUR GRAVE**. D: Micael Gast, French, 1960. W: B. Vians & J. Dopagne. C: Christian Marquano, Antonella Lualdi. Bizarre treatment of American South, complete with Negro servants and leather-jacketed motorcycle gangs, dealing with a black seeking sexual revenge for the lynching of his brother. Exemplifies French interest in U.S. race relations, as in French production **Tamango**, which deals with revolt on U.S. slave ship in early 1800s, with Captain, Curt Jurgens, conflicted due to his black mistress, Dorothy Dandridge (1958).

**THE CATCH**. Nagisa Oshima, Japanese, 1961. W: Tsutomo Tamura. P: Palace Film Productions. A black U.S. airman is captured in a small Japanese village during the last summer of World War II, and becomes a scapegoat for the villagers' psychological ills, finally being killed, as the war ends.

**ON FRIDAY AT ELEVEN**. D: Alvin Rakoff, British, 1961. W: P.A. Cruter & Frank Harvey. P: P.A. Cruter. C: Rod Steiger, Peter Van Eyck, Ian Ballen. Exemplary "international" production, in this case a crime story involving a gang which is a sort of "miniaturized

NATO" with the tough U.S. leader repeatedly challenged by the cold German crook.

**PIGS AND BATTLESHIPS.** D: Shohei Imamura, Japanese, 1961. W: Hisashi Yamauchi. P: Nikkatsu. Tragic-comic study of lowest strata of Japanese society encountering U.S. occupation forces. The lower class heroine hopes only to escape her milieu of battle-ships and mobsters, but is gangraped by U.S. soldiers, and finally dies in a bizarre shootout amid a pig stampede.

**TEARS ON THE LION'S MANE.** D: Schochiku, Japanese, 1962. W: S. Terrayama, et al. Moody counterpart to U.S. rock-rebel/rock-idol films. In a striking sequence, Japan's idol, Fujiki, raging at a betrayal, seizes his guitar and starts to wail — grotesque, comic, and moving.

**HIGH AND LOW.** D: Akira Kurasawa, Japan, 1963. W: Mr. Kura-sawa, et al. b/o Ed McBain's crime novel *King's Ransom*. P: Toho Co. C: Toshiro Mifune, Tatsuya Nakadai. Sizzling detective thriller which also deals with U.S. and western problems such as economic inequality in a business society. Prof. Joan Mellen has pointed out **High and Low** compares capitalism to war ("It's either win or lose") via the defeats of various characters.

**YOUR EXCELLENCY.** D: Cantiflas, Mexico, 1963. Cantiflas plays a U.N. ambassador from a tiny Latin nation, whose vote is crucial. Plot has one superpower, Dolaronia ("The Big Dollars"), promising collosal aid programs, the other superpower sending in a Mata Hari.

**THE LOVED ONE.** D: Tony Richardson, British, 1965. W: T. South-ern & C. Isherwood. b/o Evelyn Waugh's novel. P: Filmways, Inc. C: Robert Morse, Jonathan Winters, Rod Steiger. Offensive, artist-ically unsuccessful film based on satirical book about American funeral industry.

**ON THE SAME PLANET.** D: Ilya Olshvanger, Soviet Russian, 1965. P: Mosfilm. Post-deStalinization drama involving humane Lenin, malevolent Stalin, and centering around Lenin's contention that the U.S. can be trusted by the Soviet Union.

**HOUR OF THE FURNACES.** D: Fernando Solas, Argentina, 1965. W: Mr. Solas & Octavio Getino. A call for worldwide revolution, including extreme anti-Americanism "so strong that even Argen-tinians having a good time dancing to rock music are intercut with. . . deprivations, as if American decadence had turned them into Neros." — Pauline Kael.

**BILLION DOLLAR BRAIN**. D: Ken Russell, British, 1967. W: J. McGrath. P: Harry Saltzman. C: Michael Caine, Karl Malden, Oscar Homolka. Interesting anti-American spy "cartoon," with extremely complex plot, repellant hysterical anti-Communist Texas oil millionaire complete with private army which invades Latvia, and sympathetic Soviet government.

**FAR FROM VIETNAM**. D: Alain Resnais, William Klein, Joris Ivens, Agnes Varda, Claude Lelouch, Jean Luc Godard, largely French, 1967. P: Ston. A compilation war commentary that carries the angry message that the Vietnam War is one of the rich against the poor, and nationalist revolutions cannot be stopped.

**A FISTFUL OF DOLLARS**. D: Serge Leone, Italian, 1967. P: Jolly Films (Rome), Constantin Films (Munich), and Ocean Films (Madrid). C: Clint Eastwood. Exemplary "spaghetti western" (in truth an international production). Exaggerates all U.S. figures of style, from mysterious gunman entering evil frontier town onward. Bosley Crowther sees hero as ruthless but not cruel, fascinating but not real — a morbid, amusing, campy fraud.

**LEMONADE JOE**. D: Oldrich Lipsky, Czechoslovakian, 1967. W: Jeri Brdeca & Mr. Lipsky. P: Tele Net International. C: Karel Fiala, Olga Schberova. Deft parody of American western, with cowpokes of "Stetson City" babbling in Czech.

**MADE IN U.S.A**. W, D: Jean-Luc Godard, French, 1967. P: Anounchka Films. C: Anna Karina, Lsazlo Szabo, Jean Pierre Leaud. Highly stylized and experimental rendering of the Ben Barka affair (murder of a Left Wing journalist, possibly involving the C.I.A.). Includes many allusions to the Kennedy assassination, Americanization and U.S. imperialism. (See text.)

**POINT BLANK**. D: John Boorman, British, 1967. W: Alex Jacobs & D. & R. Newhouse. b/o Richard Stark's novel *The Hunter*. P: J. Bernard & R. Chartoff. C: Lee Marvin, Angie Dickinson, Keenan Wynn. Crime thriller as American allegory. Implacable, never-let-up hero out for what is due him, the Los Angeles setting reflecting his emptiness and alienation, his criminal activity a counterpart of modern business. (See text.)

**THE MODEL SHOP**. D, W, P: Jacques Demy, French, 1968. C: Anouk Aimee, Gary Lockwood. Demy's "loveless love story" deals with a mature Frenchwoman's brief affair with a rootless young American about to be drafted for Vietnam; a lyrical romantic story notable for showing various aspects of the American counterculture (underground newspapers, a rock group commune, unmarried couples living together). (See text.)

**BLOOD OF THE CONDOR.** D: Gorge Sanlines, Argentinian, 1969. W: Oscar Soaria & Mr. Sanlines. P: Ukamau Limitada. C: Marcelino Yanahuaya, Benedicta Huanca, Vincente Salinas. L: Tricontinential. Dramatized criticism of population control programs by U.S. "Progress Corps" in Latin America.

**DESERTER IN SWEDEN.** W, D: Lars Lambert & Oile Sjogren, Swedish, 1969. P: Lars Lambert. Three young U.S. army deserters reenact their years of foreign sanctuary.

**HUNGER FOR LOVE.** D: Nelson Pereira Dos Santos, Brazilian, 1969. L: Unitar. Self-mocking treatment of young Brazilian exiles in Greenwich Village, New York City.

**MIDNIGHT COWBOY.** D: John Schlesinger, British, 1969. W: Waldo Salt, b/o novel by James Leo Herlihy. P: Jerome Hellman–John Schlesinger. C: Dustin Hoffman, Jon Voight, Brenda Vaccaro. Like his other early films, about naive young people struggling with the complex demanding and sometimes cruel U.S. social environment, and their own self-destructive impulses. (See text.)

**ZABRISKIE POINT.** D: Michelangelo Antonioni, Italian, 1969. S: Mr. Antonioni, et al. P: Carlo Ponti. C: Mark Frechette, Daria Halprin, Rod Taylor. Antonioni's making of common cause with America's 1960s rebelling youth, attracted by their natural animal vitality, and because they know "not to calmly accept the adult vision of reality, which seems to have produced monstrous results." (See text.)

**THE AMERICAN SOLDIER.** W, D: R.W. Fassbinder, German, 1970. C: Karl Schedt, Elga Sorbas. Full scale mood-thick homage to U.S. gangster films: soft hats, white suits, and bulging shoulder holsters.

**COUNTDOWN CANADA.** W, D, P: Robert Fothergill, Canada, 1970. C: Stanley Burke, Barbara Frum. L: Canadian Filmmakers Distribution Center, Toronto. Remarkable drama dealing with the day Canada joins the U.S.A., in the form of TV coverage of the visiting president, protestors, and a defiant Canadian Liberation Front (B&W, 60 min.).

**THE DOORS TO PARADISE.** D: Salomon Laiter, Mexican, 1970. W: Elena Varco. P: Cinematografica Marte, S.A. C: Jaqueline An-

dere, Jorge Luke. Tale of Mexical middleclass young people explor-
ing the world of drugs and counterculture, suggesting how the out-
look of the new generation of Mexicans is heavily shaped and influenced by the United States.

**HISTORY OF POSTWAR JAPAN AS TOLD BY A BAR HOSTESS.**
D: Shohe Imamura, Japanese, 1970. P: Nihon Eiga Shinsha/Toho. A
a treatment of a middle-aged Japanese woman married to an American, and operating a bar for the U.S. military. She reconstructs her
own life, commenting scornfully on newsreel footage of parallel major events.

**LION'S LOVE.** W, P, D: Agnes Varda, French, 1970. C: Viva,
Jerome Ragni, James Rado, Shirley Clarke, Carlos Clarens. Varda's
experimental, highly sytlized collage of her experiences in Hollywood in 1968, which suggests a very personal view of how America's personal, political and Hollywood illustions are created and
function. (See text.)

**MYRA BRECKENRIDGE.** D: Michael Sarne, French, 1970. S:
Mr. Sarne & David Giler, b/o Gore Vidal novel. P: Robert Fryer.
C: Mae West, John Huston, Rachel Welch. Confused unsuccessful
satire of Hollywood and American sexuality.

**BORN TO WIN.** D: Ivan Passer, Czech, 1971. W: D.S. Milton. P:
Philip Langner. C: George Segal, Paula Prentice,Karen Black. Very
unsatisfactory treatment of the life of the New York City drug culture.

**COWBOYS.** D: Sami Salamai, Egyptian, 1971. L: Icarus Films. U.S.
cowboys and other action films (widely shown in the Middle East),
together with rock and roll, treated as tools of cultural penetration
and domination.

**JOE HILL.** D: Bo Widerberg, Swedish, 1971. W: Mr. Widerberg. P:
Sagittarius Productions. C: Tommy Bergueren, Anja Schmidt. Uneven, poetic treatment of Swedish-immigrant songwriter/U.S. labor
activist in the 1900s.

**HUCKLEBERRY FINN.** D: Giorgi N. Daneliya, Soviet Russian,
1971. W: Mr. Daneliya & V. Tokareva. P: Mosfilm. C: Felix Im-
mokueke, Roma Madyanov. Notable Soviet attempt to render U.S.
classic novel.

**MEDICINE BALL CARAVAN.** D: François Reichenbach, French,

1971. P: Mr. Reichenbach & Tom Donahue. Affected documentary of a U.S. counterculture cross-country bus trip by musicians, beautiful people, the Hog Farm, and so on.

**PUNISHMENT PARK**. D: Peter Watkins, British, 1971. P: Susan Martin for Francois Films. C: Jim Bohan, Van Daniels. Intense, sincere masochistic sci-fi film of future U.S., in which anti-Vietnam protestors must demonstrate their loyalty via an impossible desert endurance race.

**REDU TAKH**. D: Mahama Traore, Senegal, 1971. L: Uni-film. Young Afro-Americans visit Africa in search of their roots. Includes discussions with Senegalese students on contemporary Africa's significance for Afro-Americans.

**SACCO AND VANZETTI**. D: Giuliano Montaldo, Italian, 1971. W: Fabrizio Onogri & Mr. Montaldo. P: Hardy Columbo & George Pappi. C: Glan Maria Volonto, Riccardo Cucciolla. Condemned as another left wing European blast at the U.S.; praised as calling attention to a terrible chapter in U.S. history. Joan Baez sings the "Ballad of Sacco and Vanzetti."

**TAKING OFF**. D: Milos Forman, Czech, 1971. W: Mr. Forman, et al. P: Alfred W. Crown. C: Lynn Carlin, Buck Henry, Linnea Heacock. A comic drama about middleclass parents in search of their teenage runaway, filmed in the gentle mocking manner of Forman's previous comedies. (See text.)

**FAREWELL UNCLE TOM**. W, P: Franco Prosperi & G. Valtiero Jacopetti, Italian-European, 1972. L: Cannon Releasing Corp. An exploitation "documentary" on American racism, including slaveships, slave breeding farms, and caged blacks used for scientific research, concluding with modern blacks butchering middleclass whites in their homes.

**LADY LIBERTY**. D: Mario Manicelli, Italian, 1972. P: United Artists. C: William Devine, Sophia Loren. Italian immigrant girl (Loren) attempts to enter the U.S. and is ensnarled in red tape.

**ONE WAY**. W, D: Jorde Darnell, Mexican, 1972. P: Vogue Films, Roma-Italia, Estudios. C: Fernando Rey, Mimsy Farmer. Life and death of Latin Americans who cross the border to work in the United States.

**SUMMER SOLDIERS**. D: Hiroshi Teshighara, Japanese, 1972. W:

John Nathan. P: Teshigahara Productions. C: Keith Sykes, Lee Reisen. Levelheaded, intelligent treatment of young U.S. soldier trying to desert on leave from Vietnam in Japan; a witty, affecting anti-war film.

**TAKE TWO.** W, P, D: Baruch Dienar. P: Take Two Productions. C: Oren Levy, Sherry Ren-Smith. Story of "swinging" Israeli cameraman Assi Doran, who takes on idealistic U.S. hippie assistant Kimmy-Lee Jones, whose constant criticism of his "commercial trash" leads to their falling in love. Exemplifies "love-hate theme" in Israeli movies which involve the U.S.: **Whisper My Name** (1971) has U.S. stewardess revitalized by Kibbutz life; **Day of Judgement** (1974) involves Israeli husband running off with U.S. tourist, but returning for Six Day War; **Neither by Day nor by Night** (1967) has blinded U.S. volunteer in Israel learning new strength.

**ALLIANCE FOR PROGRESS.** W, P, D: Julio Luduenva, Bolivian, 1973. L: Tricontinental. Radical political allegory of Latin American life, whose characters include The Businessman, The Priest, The General, and the stunningly beautiful woman called U.S.A., who wants to grind up Latin cities into foundation stone to build super-highways for which she would then sell cars.

**THE EMIGRANTS** and **THE NEW LAND.** D: Jan Troell, Swedish, 1973. W: Bengt Forslund and Mr. Troell. P: Mr. Forslund. C: Max von Sydow, Liv Ullman. Epic two-part film on Swedish migration to the United States, including a lyrical sense of the natural untamed American environment, and how it shaped us.

**THE HARDER THEY COME.** D, P: Perry Henzel, Jamaican, 1973. W: Mr. Henzel and T.D. Rhone. C: Jimmy Cliff, Janet Barkley, Carl Bradshaw. Focuses on a young Jamaican singer, but includes much material on Americanization of Jamaica, including drug trade and music industry reshaping the local economy and folkways.

**LAST TANGO IN PARIS.** D: Bernardo Bertolucci, Italian, 1973. W: Mr. Bertolucci and F. Arcalli. P: Albert Grimaldi. C: Marlon Brando, Maria Schneider. A significant artistic treatment of the arch-typical American loner/lover/rebel *in extremis*. Note for instance that the Brando character's description of his past is the list of his film roles.

**STATE OF SIEGE.** D: Costas-Gavras, Greek, 1973. W: Franco Solinas & Mr. Costas-Gavras. P: J. Perrin. C: Yves Montand, Renato Salvatore. Powerful fictionalization of kidnapping and execution of a U.S. citizen advisor to the A.I.D. police programs in Latin America, as well as the U.S. policies which led to local abuse ("U.S. historical role as Big Daddy in Latin America" — *New York Times*.

**LONG LIVE THE REPUBLIC!** W, D: Pastor Vega, Cuban, 1973. P: Cuban Film Institute. D: Unitar. Cuban Film Institute compilation documentary of Cuba history, emphasizing U.S. "colonization," up to Cuba's 1950s role as a laboratory for the consumer society.

**WILLOW SPRINGS.** W, D: Werner Schroeter, German, 1973. C: Magdalena Montezuma, Christina Kaufman. An extremely stylized film of individuals acting out their rituralistic relationships in the context of Western and U.S. values and culture. Figures move abstractly across the Mojave Desert, to a background of tragic arias, country western ballads, and 1950s rock.

**MADE IN GERMANY AND U.S.A.** P, D, W: Rudolph Thome, German, 1974. C: Karin Thome, Alf Bold. Film set in the 1930s about a German couple experiencing marital problems who separate, go to New York City, and are eventually reconciled. Highly stylized; half documentary and half fiction.

**THE OUTSIDE MAN.** D: Jaques Deray, French, 1974. C: Jean Louis Triginiant, Anne Margaret, Angie Dickinson. Gangster thriller set in Los Angeles. Notable for a rich sense of background, as well as a knowing treatment of the U.S. genre, e.g., the final shootout is in a mortuary.

**ALICE IN THE CITIES.** W, D: Wim Wenders, German, 1975. P: Peter Genee. C: Yella Rottlander & Rudiger Vgeler. Story of a German journalist's extensive trip through the U.S., Germany, and Holland, whose meanings include a political commentary on the American cultural hegemony.

**THE PASSENGER.** D: Michelangelo Antonioni, Italian, 1975. W: Mr. Antonioni, et al. P: Metro-Goldwyn-Mayer. C: Jack Nicholson, Maria Schneider. In Nicholson, Antonioni finds the personification of the indolence, listless charm, and faded resolution of contemporaneous America.

**AMERICAN FRIEND.** D: Wim Wenders, German, 1977. W: Mr. Wenders, b/o P. Highsmith's *Ripley's Game*. P: Road Movies. C: Brune Ganz, Dennis Hopper. Like all his films, undercurrent is the Americanization of Germany, most obviously in the plot of an American hoodlum corrupting a German craftsman.

**FROM THE EARTH TO THE MOON.** A, P, D: Boubaker Adjali, Algerian, 1977. L: Icarus Films. A documentary treating the nationalization of U.S. and other foreign facilities by Third World countries as a "sacred right" — the protection of local resources and economies.

**THE LIFE OF ROSE.** W, D: Hans-Christof Stenzel, German, 1977. P: Rosemarie Stenzel-Qast. C: Ms. Stenzel-Qast, John Cage. Story of Rose S. Levy, also called Claire or Fischerge, and his(her) efforts to survive in the United States.

**PROOF OF THE MAN.** D: Junya Sato, Japanese, 1977. W: Zewzo Matsuyama. P: Kadokawa. C: George Kennedy, Toshiro Mifume, Broderick Crawford. Fast-moving murder mystery resembling U.S. thriller which races from New York's Harlem to Tokyo, dealing with a black-Nipponese youth. Typifies mindless use of foreign backgrounds in transnational productions.

**STROZEK.** W, P, D: Werner Herzog, German, 1977. C: Bruno Stroszek, Eva Mattes, Clemmens Schiez. Bruno S., the basic Herzog character, is transplanted from Berlin to Wisconsin's farm country with a comely whore and a stoical friend. Film devices emphasize their estrangement, and futile attempts to change this inner stasis in the U.S. environment, making the latter seem especially cruel, bizarre, and capricious.

**WOMEN IN NEW YORK.** W, D, P: Fassbinder, West German, 1977, b/o the play "The Women," by C.B. Luce. C: Margit Carstensen, Eva Mattes. Luce's Depression Era cosmopolites from a modernist angle; a dissection of a male-oriented, class-constructed society which so oppresses women they must exploit each other to survive.

**I OFTEN REMEMBER HAWAII.** D: Elfi Mikesh, German, 1978. P: Filmwelt Verleih. C: Carmen, Ruth & Tito Rossol. An experimental mixture of documentary and dramatized fiction describing the life of a sixteen-year-old German girl.

**FLAMING HEARTS.** W, D: Walter Bochmayer, Rolf Buhrmann. P: Enten Produkton. C: Peter Kerno, Barbara Valentin. The owner of a small Bavarian newsstand wins a trip to New York City, meets a German striptease artist down on her luck, and a comic romance ensues.

**MISSILE X — THE NEUTRON BOMB INCIDENT.** D: Leslie Martinson, German, 1978. W: Clark Reynolds & Eio Romano. P: Eichberg

Film/Cinelux Romano Film. C: Kurt Jurgens, Peter Graves. The U.S. and Soviet Union work together to foil a terrorist group who have their own neutron bomb.

**FLEISCH**. W, D: Rainer Erler, German, 1979. P: Penta Grramma, Munchen. C: Jutta Speidel, Wolf Roth. While honeymooning in the U.S., a young German couple is kidnapped by a gang specializing in killing people, and selling their healthy internal organs for medical transplant operations.

**THE SUPER (EL SUPER)**. D: Leon Ichaso & Orlando Jiminez Leal, Cuban, 1979. C: Raymond Hidalgo Cato, Zulla Montero. A ten-year Cuban exile's comic struggles in New York City, a strange land of snow, garbage and crime.

**ATLANTIC CITY**. W: John Guare. P: International Film Corp. D: Louis Malle. French, 1980. C: Burt Lancaster, Susan Sarandon. On one level an implausible Hollywood thriller about drug dealing and gangland killings, in truth a poignantly sad rendering of America's cultural and material landscape.

**MY ROAD**. D: Kiuki Kawaskai. P: Kazuo Kuroi, Manny Scheffler. 1981(?). C: Leslie Winston. Two Japanese, in the U.S. as tourists, meet accidentally and travel west. A "road story" as an intelligent, serious treatment of cultural "cross pollination," produced by a major Japanese film critic.

---

**HAMMETT**. D: Wim Wenders, German, 1982(?). W: Joe Gores, et al. b/9 Gores' novel. P: Zoetrope Studios. C: Frederic Forest, Ronee Blakley. Stylized treatment of biography of the U.S. creator of hardboiled detective story, who was himself a private detective.

**JOHN REED (MEXICO IN FLAMES; OCTOBER; I SAW THE NEW WORLD BORN)**. D: Sergei Bondachuck, Soviet Russian, 1982. W: Mickey Knox, b/o Reed's *Insurgent Mexico* and *Ten Days That Shook the World*. C: Franco Nero, Sydne Rome. A full-scale, detailed depiction of the events of the Russian Revolution in three parts, using two attractive westerners as interpreters and observers.

**MISSING**. D: Costa Gavras, Greek, French. S.P.: C.G. and Donald Stuart, b/o *Missing* by Thomas Hauser. P: Edward Lewis & Mildred Lewis. C: Jack Lemmon, Sissy Spacek. Political melodrama of 1973 kidnapping and murder of young U.S. journalist in Chile, possibly with complicity of U.S. officials.

# References

## Chapter 1

1.1    Antonioni, M. "Let's Talk about Zabriskie Point." *Esquire*, New York, August, 1970.

1.2    Burkes, John. "Fourteen Points to Zabriskie Point." *Rolling Stone*, New York, March 7, 1970.

13.    Callenbach, Ernest. "Zabriskie Point." *Film Quarterly*, Berkeley, California, Spring, 1970.

1.4    Cohen, Larry. "Dreaming America." *University Review*, New York, March, 1970.

1.5    Cohen, Larry. "Interview with Antonioni." *University Review*, New York, March, 1970.

1.6    Flaherty, Guy. "I Love This Country." *The New York Times*, New York, February 28, 1970.

1.7    Goldstein, Richard. "Did Antonioni Miss the 'Point'?" *The New York Times*, New York, February 22, 1970.

1.8    Jebb, Julian. "Intimations of Reality: Getting the Zabriskie Point." *Sight & Sound*, London, Summer, 1970.

1.9    Kael, Pauline. "The Beauty of Destruction." *The New Yorker*, February 21, 1970.

1.10    *L'Avventura: A Film by Michelangelo Antonioni*. Grove Press, Inc., New York, 1969.

1.11    Sarris, Andrew. "Films in Focus." *The Village Voice*, New York, February 12, 1970.

1.11    Zavatsky, Bill. "Plastic America." *University Review*, New York, March, 1970.

## Chapter 2

2.1    Brown, John Lindsay. "Island of the Mind." *Sight and Sound*, 39, Winter 1969/70, 20–23.

2.2    Farber, Stephen. "The Writer in American Films I." *Film Quarterly*, 21, Summer 1968, 2–13.

2.3    Farber, Stephen. "The Writer in American Films: An Interview with Alexander Jacobs." *Film Quarterly*, 21, Fall/Winter 1968–69, 2–13.

2.4    French, Philip. "Point Blank." *Sight and Sound*, 38, Spring, 1968, 98.

2.5    Martin, James Mitchell. "Point Blank." *Film Quarterly*, 21, Summer, 1968, 40–43.

2.6    Ross, T.J. "Point Blank: A Stalker in the City." *Film Heritage*, 5, Fall, 1969, 21–26.

## Chapter 3

3.1    Canby, Vincent. "Model Shop Looks Out on Los Angeles." *The New York Times*, February 12, 1969.

3.2    Delahaye, Michael. "Lola in L.A.: An Interview with Jacques Demy." *Cahiers du Cinema* (reprinted in *Evergreen Review*, April, 1969, 29).

3.3    Gillet, John. "Model Shop." *Sight & Sound*, London, Spring, 1970.

3.4    Kael, Pauline. "The Lady from across the Sea: The Current Cinema." *The New Yorker*, March 14, 1969.

3.5    Mosk. "Model Shop." *Variety*, New York, January 15, 1969.

3.6    Sarris, Andrew. "Films." *The Village Voice*, February 13, 1969.

3.7    Scheuer, Philip K. "Frenchman in Hollywood." *Action*, November-December, 1968.

# Chapter 4

4.1    Benoit, Shelly. "Prototype for Hollywood's New Freedom: An Interview with Universal's Ned Tanen." *Show*, March, 1971, v2 n1, p24.

4.2    Canby, Vincent. "Taking Off: Milos Forman Directs a Charming Farce." *The New York Times*, March 29, 1971, p40.

4.3    Crist, Judith. "Doesn't Anyone Play Parcheesi Anymore?" *New York Magazine*, April 5, 1971, p60,61.

4.4    Forman, Milos. "How I Came to America to Make a Film and Wound Up Owing Paramount $140,000." *Show*, February, 1970, v1 n2.

4.5    Gilliatt, Penelope. "The Current Cinema: A Fist, with the Hand Itself." *The New Yorker*, April 3, 1971, p107–109.

4.6    Haskell, Molly. "Film: Downfall Parents." *The Village Voice*, April 1, 1971, p71,74.

4.7    Hatch, Robert. "Taking Off." *The Nation*, April 19, 1971.

4.8    Kagan, Norman. "An Interview with Milos Forman." (unpublished), January 11, 1971.

4.9    Murf. "Taking Off." *Variety*, March 17, 1971, p18.

4.10   Polt, Harriet. "Getting the Great Ten Per Cent: An Interview with Milos Forman." *Film Comment*, v6 n3, Fall, 1970.

4.11   Production notes on **Taking Off** from Billings Associates, 200 W. 57th St., New York, New York.

4.12   Schickel, Richard. "Parents and Kids with Orgies." *Life*, April 12, 1971, p12.

4.13   Weiler, A.H. " 'Dropping Out' with Milos Forman." *The New York Times*, October 20, 1968.

4.14   Winston, Archer. "Taking Off Opens at the Plaza." *The New York Post*, Monday, March 29, 1971, p20.

4.15   *Women's Wear Daily* interview with Milos Forman.

# Chapter 5

5.1    Bagehot, Henry. "Who Kidnapped Ben Barka?" *Made in U.S.A.* (screenplay), by Jean-Luc Godard.

5.2    Cameron, Ian. "Made in U.S.A." in *The Films of Jean Luc Godard*, ed. by Ian Cameron, Studio-Vista, London, 1969.

5.3    Ehrenstein, David. "Festival Feedback." *The Village Voice*, October 12, 1967.

5.4    Godard, Jean-Luc. "The Left and Made in U.S.A." *Made in U.S.A.: The Screenplay*, by Jean-Luc Godard.

5.5    Godard, Jean-Luc. *Made in U.S.A.: The Screenplay*. Corrimer Publishing, London, 1967.

5.6    Federman, Raymond. "Jean-Luc Godard and Americanism." *Film Heritage*, v3 n3, Spring, 1968.

5.7    Karol, K.S. "The Ben Barka Fiasco." in *Made in U.S.A.: The Screenplay*, by Jean-Luc Godard.

5.8    Kernan, Margaret. "Made in U.S.A." in *Film Heritage*, v3 n3, Spring, 1968.

5.9    Kustow, K.S. "Introduction." in *Made in U.S.A.: The Screenplay*, bv Jean-Luc Godard.

5.10   McBean, James Roy. "Politics, Painting, and the Language of Signs in Godard's Made in U.S.A." *Film Quarterly*, v 22 n3, Spring, 1968.

5.11   Roud, Richard. *Godard*. Doubleday & Co., Garden City, New York, 1968.

# Chapter 6

6.1    Canby, Vincent. "Midnight Cowboy." *The New York Times*, May 25, 1969.

6.2    Crist, Judith. "Mourning at Midnight." *New York Magazine*, June 2, 1969, p48.

6.3    Dawson, Jan. "Midnight Cowboy." *Sight & Sound*, Autumn, 1969, v34 n4, p211.

6.4    Denby, David. "Midnight Cowboy." *Film Quarterly*, Fall, 1969, v23 n1.

6.5    Farber, Stephen. "End of the Road." *Film Quarterly*, Winter, 1969-70, v23 n2, p3.

6.6    Geimis, Joseph. "Cowboy Strong, Unconvincing." *Newsday*, May 25, 1969, p24.

6.7    Herlihy, James Leo. *Midnight Cowboy*. Simon & Schuster, New York, 1965.

6.8    Kael, Pauline. "Life, Love, Death, Etc. . . . " *The New Yorker*, May 31, 1969.

6.9    Land. "Midnight Cowboy." *Variety*, May 14, 1969.

6.10   Phillips, Gene. "John Schlesinger, Social Realist." *Film Comment*, v5 n4, Winter, 1969, p58.

6.11   Reed, Rex. "Movies." *Women's Wear Daily*, May 26, 1969; June 18, 1969.

6.12   Rossell, Deac. "Riding into the Sunset of Harsh Reality." *New England Summer Preview*, 1969.

## Chapter 7

7.1    Canby, Vincent. "Film Fete: Viva, Ragni and Ado in Lion's Love." *The New York Times*, September 22, 1969.

7.2    Haskell, Molly. "Film: Lion's Love." *The Village Voice*, October 23, 1969.

7.3    Hoops, Jonathan. "Lion's Love." *Film Quarterly*, Summer, 1970, p60.

7.4    Mekas, Jonas. "Movie Journal." *The Village Voice*, October 16, 1969.

7.5    Thompson, Howard. "Woman Born on 'New Wave' " in *The New York Times*, May, 1967.

7.6    Varda, Agnes. "Varda on Lion's Love." PR release.

**Norman Kagan**, M.F.A., Ph.D. candidate (Columbia University, New York City) is writer-producer of over 150 informational films, including four years of **U.S.I.A. Science Report**, seen on television in 110 countries worldwide. His books include *The Cinema of Stanley Kubrick*, *The War Film*, *Greenhorns: Foreign Filmmakers Interpret America*, and *American Skeptic: Robert Altman's Genre-Commentary Films*. He is a member of the Association of Independent Video and Filmmakers, the American Science Film Association (secretary-trustee), the Informational Film Producers Association, the National Science Writers Association, and the University Film Association.